Anthropology and Food Policy

Anthropology and Food Policy

Human Dimensions of Food Policy in Africa and Latin America

Della E. McMillan, Editor
With the assistance of Jeanne Harlow

Southern Anthropological Society Proceedings, No. 24
Mary W. Helms, Series Editor

The University of Georgia Press
Athens and London

Southern Anthropological Society

Founded 1966

© 1991 by the Southern Anthropological Society
Published by the University of Georgia Press
Athens, Georgia 30602
All rights reserved
Set in Times Roman
The paper in this book meets the guidelines for
permanence and durability of the Committee on
Production Guidelines for Book Longevity of the
Council on Library Resources.

Printed in the United States of America

95   94   93   92   91   5   4   3   2   1

Library of Congress Cataloging in Publication Data

Anthropology and food policy : human dimensions of food policy in
    Africa and Latin America / Della E. McMillan, editor, with the
    assistance of Jeanne Harlow.
        p. cm.—(Southern Anthropological Society proceedings ; no. 24)
        Includes bibliographical references (p.   ).
        ISBN 0-8203-1287-8 (alk. paper).—ISBN 0-8203-1288-6 (pbk. :
    alk. paper)
        1. Nutrition policy—Africa.   2. Nutrition policy—Latin America.
    3. Applied anthropology—Africa.   4. Applied anthropology—Latin
    America.   I. McMillan, Della E.   II. Harlow, Jeanne.   III. Series.
    GN2.S9243 no. 24
    [TX360.A26]
    301 s—dc20
    [363.8′096]   90-11000
                                       CIP

British Library Cataloging in Publication Data available

To Ronald Cohen
gentle mentor of many anthropologists in food policy

Contents

Introduction

Della E. McMillan

Why study food policy? From the 1960s to the 1970s the world exalted in the original promise and performance of the Green Revolution, which produced spectacular increases in many staple food crops in Asia and Latin America. Many observers were optimistic that the gross shortcomings in world food production would soon be ended. Unfortunately, as the decade of the 1980s developed, these increases slowed and in the face of continued population growth, distortions in world food supplies resumed their former prominence. For many policymakers, the problem lay in developing still more sophisticated production techniques. For others the complexity of the world's social, political, and economic systems suggested that there were many more variables that had to be considered before the problem of hunger and malnutrition could be solved.

Food policy developed either by nations or international organizations, in the view of a new generation of researchers, has to include not only the multiple aspects of production but also the multiple effects of distribution patterns stemming from individual national policies, international food trade competition, the availability and use of food aid, social class, cultural biases and conflicts, and the operations of different types of markets. In addition, a wide variation in consumption patterns and preferences was related to conditions of health and well-being, age and gender, social and cultural conflict, and classic rural-urban divisions within populations.

With such an extraordinarily complex range of variables, something more is needed before an effective worldwide system of policies can be developed to manage both individual national and international food problems. It is a task that cannot be solved by one discipline alone but requires the collaborative effort of motivated researchers working from grassroots levels to computerized think tanks, from field anthropologists to the most esoteric of macroeconomic analysts. This volume is an attempt to move in that direction.

The idea for the volume grew out of a recognized need in applied anthropology for researchers to have a better understanding of the perspectives of their anthropologist and sociologist colleagues working in different areas of domestic U.S. and international food policy. The book is intended neither to provide a complete review of the anthropological writings in the field nor to make a definitive statement about what the role of anthropology in food policy analysis has, will, or ought to be. Rather, our goal was to bring together writings by anthropologists in the main subject areas of supply/production, distribution, and consumption. This collection should be viewed as a companion volume to two excellent reviews of food policy issues that have recently been published by the World Bank. The first, *Food Policy Analysis* (Timmer, Falcon, and Pearson 1983), presents the tools and analytical frameworks for doing the types of economic analyses that provide the foundation of food policy analysis. The second volume, *Food Policy: Integrating Supply, Distribution and Consumption* (Gittinger, Leslie, and Hoisington 1987), is more interdisciplinary and includes thirty-nine chapters by economists, anthropologists, agronomists, nutritionists, and political scientists. The articles provide an excellent overview of the international framework of food policy analysis as well as more specialized concerns with agricultural production, marketing, price policies, subsidies, malnutrition, and nutrition interventions. The edited volume by Gittinger, Leslie, and Hoisington is especially useful to nonspecialists who wish to increase their familiarity with the issues.

The chapters here provide a valuable sociocultural perspective on the broad policy issues concerning supply, distribution, and consumption that are discussed in the other two collections. By starting from a base of extensive anthropological fieldwork in particular societies and communities, the authors utilize case studies to examine the meaning of their findings for the understanding needed for specific policy interventions. Thus an anthropologist can talk about food preferences and how malnourishment occurs within a family or community context and can raise questions from this base about the nature of national and international food policies which, unknown to local consumers, directly affect their well-being and, indeed, their social and political lives.

One important aspect of studying food and hunger at the grassroots is that one quickly discovers that most people have no understanding of the nature of the policies—or even the existence of the policies—which by and large determine how and what they eat. Individuals have one perspective on the problem if they are farmers and produce most of what their families eat; they have an entirely different perspective if they are urban consumers and must purchase what they consume. Local people have virtually no idea what determines the prices they receive for their products or the types of food they find in the marketplace. Also impressive is the fact that these same local people have virtually no participation in the policy-making process that determines market prices and products. The autocratic nature of decisions made by policy elites, who determine the nature, cost, and variety of the family food basket, would seem anachronistic in light of the explosive contemporary development of participatory governments and movements throughout the world. It seems to the authors in this volume that for people to take a more active role in determining what food policies they want, a more adequate foundation of information and analysis is necessary.

Food policy is not simply a matter that rests in the offices of international banks and organizations but in fact is ultimately developed by members of households who themselves must go out and make choices about what types of food they will purchase—how much and what kind. Whoever purchases food is making policy decisions. These choices are based on patterns and preferences as well as individual perceptions of what they and their families may require to be adequately nourished.

We are talking about a food policy chain or pyramid. If someone at the top of the pyramid makes a decision that the people in a given country will eat cheap, imported wheat at a given market price, the food decisions of consumers and local policymakers are affected all down the pyramid. The local people were not involved in the macro-level policy decision that is resulting in the imported wheat being sold at a cheaper price than more nutritious, locally produced food staples like potatoes and corn. Their own purchases, however, and, if they are producers, decisions about what to plant are influenced by the lower price for imported wheat.

We hope this book will be used to stimulate discussion, interest, and research on the many important issues that face world policymakers, and in particular we hope that it will stimulate anthropologists to turn their attention to this vital field. It is a topic which has biblical proportions and one that involves every human society and culture, being brought together by the complexity of world systems.

ORGANIZATION OF THE CHAPTERS

The chapters in the volume are organized to reflect a general overview of food policy concerns and the three major divisions in food policy analysis: supply/production, distribution, and consumption.

The first chapter, by Billie DeWalt and David Barkin, is a graphic illustration of the potential dangers of a development policy that focuses singly on increased production. The chapter describes the spectacular success of new Green Revolution technology in raising Mexico's production of wheat and sorghum. Despite the fact that by 1980 grain production in Mexico was eight times what it was in 1940, while population only trebled, large numbers of rural and urban people remain seriously malnourished. One reason for this condition is the fact that with existing technology and price policies, farmers are encouraged to grow feed for livestock rather than table food. While poorer Mexicans may occasionally consume livestock products such as milk and eggs, the distribution of these products is sharply skewed towards the upper- and middle-income groups.

Crop and Livestock Production

The second two chapters, by Art Hansen and Terrence McCabe, emphasize various local or "human" aspects of crop and livestock production systems that are relevant to a broad-based food policy. A central theme in both chapters is the critical importance of identifying the unique needs and goals of low-income rural, producer households. Low-income households are usually those most nutritionally at risk.

Hansen's chapter uses research he conducted as part of an interdisciplinary farming systems research and extension project (FSR/E) in Malawi to examine the critical importance of recognizing heterogeneity among peasant farmers. Differences in land, labor, and cash resources as well as entrepreneurial ability are not always obvious to outside observers. While not obvious, these differences influence the willingness and ability of smallholders to adopt certain types of new crop production technology. Policymakers wishing to have an impact on the poorest households must therefore be sensitive to the special needs, concerns, and capacities of these lower income groups.

In Hansen's work the farming systems model relies heavily on farmer participation in the design, testing, and extension of new crop production technology as well as interdisciplinary collaboration of social scientists such as economists and anthropologists with specialists in the more familiar crop research sciences like agronomy, soil science, and agricultural engineering. FSR/E has today become more or less mainstream and is actively supported by the International Agricultural Research Centers (IARCs), major donors such as the World Bank and USAID, and a large number of national governments in Africa and Latin America.

McCabe contrasts the significant role that anthropologists like Hansen have played in crop-oriented research and extension with the virtual exclusion of anthropologists from any significant policy role in livestock development programs in Africa. He is especially concerned with the special problems of developing East African pastoral livestock production systems.

Pastoralism is a highly specialized subsistence strategy that is adapted to Africa's huge expanses of arid and semiarid land. The ecological conditions in much of this area are unsuitable for cultivation or sedentarization. These are the same zones that were worst hit by the well-known famines of 1968–74 and 1983–84. Efforts to promote a balanced use of Africa's land resources must therefore facilitate the development of higher yielding production systems for pastoral production as well as systems for agriculturalists.

McCabe argues that one reason for the persistent failure of livestock development projects in the area is that few programs have taken the existing livestock management systems as their point of departure, despite the demonstrated environmental soundness of certain indigenous livestock practices. Anthropologists have generally had little influence on policymakers and development planners to orient development projects to address the needs and desires of the pastoral people themselves. Instead, the anthropological input into these projects has typically been limited to documenting the repeated failures of earlier projects.

Regional Distribution and Market Systems

While an emphasis on production and trade may result in adequate food supplies, successful production and trade does not in and of itself guarantee adequate nutritional status for the population as a whole. Marketing bottlenecks, ranging from inefficient government marketing boards to the lack of basic infrastructure such as roads, bridges, and efficient telecommunications, may affect food availability (Gittinger, Leslie, and Hoisington 1987). Distribution networks may also be inadequate to cope with redistributing food supplies from grain surplus to grain deficit regions, a process which must occur very rapidly in famine years.

Economists have developed several techniques which they use to assess market efficiency—the conditions that must be met for food to be moved from producers to consumers in a timely fashion and at lowest cost. In general, however, these techniques rely on fairly accurate information on price movements and the costs of transportation, storage, and the profit margins of middlemen.

Under rural conditions in Africa and Latin America, it is difficult to acquire accurate price information on many of these topics. Reeves argues that microlevel research can reveal indirect measures of some of the same sorts of phenomena that economists have traditionally studied based on unreliable price information. Reeves suggests that the anthropologist's understanding of how food markets actually work, who the participants are, and how marketing agents acquire working capital and how marketing agents, producers, and consumers acquire information about prices can help governments design more effective policies to relieve areas of actual or projected market inefficiency.

Linking Consumption to Production and Distribution

Unfortunately, increased food production and its availability in regional markets does not guarantee that food is being consumed by those who need it most. In terms of production, poor rural people often do not have the cash or land resources to benefit from new production technology. Additionally, poor families may not have the resources to make their demand for food effective—that is, they may not have the resources to attract food to their households. In terms of consumption, the food purchases made by poor urban and rural families must compete with a host of other competing demands—for shelter, education, clothing, medical care, and consumer products.

Poverty is undoubtedly the root cause of most hunger and malnutrition in Latin America and Africa, and there are no easy solutions to the problem of poverty. Even the most optimistic assessments for future income growth foresee that the growth in real income among the poorest segments of the population will occur only slowly (Gittinger, Leslie, and Hoisington 1987). Therefore, any balanced program for national food policy must include strong complementary programs that have the explicit goal of improving the food consumption of the poor and other groups (e.g., pregnant mothers and infant children), who are considered to be at greatest nutritional risk. Nutritional risk is defined as "the chance of death, ill health, malfunction, poor achievement in body size, or hunger due to insufficient food" (McLean 1987:393). An essential feature of nutritional interventions is the identification of the type of household in which deprivation occurs (ibid.). Without understanding the context in which nutrition problems arise, governments cannot design strategies to deal with such problems.

The chapter by Baer highlights the fact that targeting households for nutritional interventions on the basis of income alone will ignore many households who are at higher income levels but just as much at nutritional risk. Significant differences exist between households in the quantity and quality of foods consumed that cannot be explained by differences in income or other measures of economic status.

Baer argues that income allocation patterns are often overlooked. There is no guarantee that the income entering households will be used for food purchases. According to Baer, policymakers can more effectively model the relationship between income growth and nutritional incomes by addressing the factors which determine "available income" as opposed to total income. The concept of available income refers to the amount of money which is actually available to those in the household who are responsible for household expenditures, including food. In most of the world, household structure is such that total income and available income are very different. Baer's research suggests that the cultural factors that influence who works and the culturally acceptable ways of disposing of the money earned are sometimes more important than total income levels in determining the nutritional result of higher or lower income households.

Consumption studies generally focus on urban households, yet one of the nagging paradoxes of food policy is that the greatest proportion of the hungry are found in rural, agricultural communities.

Dramatic increases in food and cash crop production have often not had positive impacts on the food consumption or nutrition of rural people. Projects often fail to reach the rural poor. Generally, the farmers who already have the greatest cash, land, and labor resources are best able to benefit from project activities and new technology. In addition, new technology and increased commercialization almost always bring about a reorganization of production activities. This reorganization in turn sets in motion a series of other changes in distribution and consumption, especially food consumption. Many of these changes adversely affect the welfare and nutritional status of low-income, limited-resource households and of women.

Kathleen DeWalt argues that for agricultural research and development to have a positive impact on the food consumption and nutrition of the rural poor, policymakers must make improving nutritional status an explicit goal. A review of efforts by the International Agricultural Research Centers demonstrates that most of the IARCs include improvement of nutrition as a goal of their research. Similarly, improved nutrition for the farm family was listed as a goal in the majority of small farm focused research and development projects for USAID. However, neither the IARCs nor the greater part of the USAID projects include explicit strategies for addressing nutrition concerns in project planning or implementation, nor do they include food consumption parameters in evaluation. Policymakers fall prey to the same disciplinary subdivisions described earlier. Many scientists involved in the design of these projects simply do not have the background or training to design the strategies that are needed to implement interdisciplinary or complementary programs.

The unique contribution of DeWalt's research, and other research that she has conducted in a team setting (*see* Frankenburger 1985), is the development of simple guidelines to assist policymakers with the identification of potential nutrition constraints and opportunities in development projects as well as with analysis of the potential effects of projects on the food consumption and nutrition of limited-resource farmers.

Food Aid, Trade, and Consequences

Hopkins (1987) observes that two major political forces in the early 1950s led to the creation of permanent food aid programs as a strategy for dealing with malnutrition and hunger in less-developed countries. First, agricultural groups in the United States and Canada promoted food aid as a way to expand trade and reduce burdensome grain surpluses. Second, humanitarian and internationalist sentiments had an interest in ending famine and nutritional deprivation through government funding of supplementary food aid and subsidized trade programs. The results were "a marriage of surplus disposal and humanitarian relief as a successor to the American food relief efforts in Europe following World War II" (ibid.). Since then, food aid has become institutionalized as a familiar form of international food transfers.

Doughty provides a general overview of the postwar food aid and subsidized trade programs in Latin America. He notes that since the Second World War, the U.S. has emerged as the preeminent source of imported and aid food grains in Latin America. His argument is twofold. First, in the Latin American case, the political use of food aid has taken precedence over food and development needs. In this context, the worldwide pattern is for poorer countries to have less comparative advantage in obtaining food than middle- and upper-income countries. Secondly, U.S. food aid has achieved neither its political nor its humanitarian goals. Instead, food aid and cheap food imports have tended to benefit the wealthier urban consumers who eat such products. For example, by making wheat products cheap, U.S. aid and import policies have contributed to a switch in dietary preferences of urban residents away from traditional and locally produced staples like corn and potatoes to wheat products. Doughty also argues that the availability of cheap food has in some cases encouraged governments to pay insufficient attention to the development of smallholder agriculture in the rural areas that have traditionally produced the bulk of food staples. Indeed, by worsening the plight of the poor, smallholder farmers, food aid may inadvertently have contributed to the low incomes that are often at the base of rural political unrest in the Latin American countries.

SUMMARY

To summarize, the authors in the volume address the broader issues surrounding supply, distribution, and consumption. Failure to consider the linkages between macrolevel interventions like national trade and prices, and rural and urban producers and consumers, can have a host of undesirable consequences for food systems. Yet tradeoffs between relative benefits and costs of different policies are inevitable. Addressing these constraints requires policymakers and analysts to simultaneously address the issues of food supply, distribution, and consumption at different levels of the national food system. It is our sincere belief that anthropology as a discipline, and anthropologists as trained professionals, have an important role to play in orienting future food policies so that the needs and concerns of the rural and urban poor are more adequately represented through all levels of the food policy pyramid.

ACKNOWLEDGMENTS

The history of this volume is heavily rooted in the history of the Applied Anthropology Program at the University of Kentucky, which is the oldest applied anthropology program still in operation in the country. In 1985–86, its faculty began to explore ways to strengthen dialogue across the different research groups focused on production, distribution, and consumption. One result was the creation in 1987 of a weekly faculty-student seminar called Anthropology and Food Policy. Many of the chapters presented in this volume were first conceptualized, if not delivered, in that seminar. The actual chapters were presented as part of the keynote symposium at the annual meetings of the Southern Anthropological Society in April 1989. Susan Abbott is to be thanked for encouraging us to expand some of the seminar topics into chapters in this book.

I am deeply endebted to Billie DeWalt and John Van Willigen at the University of Kentucky for their more or less forcing me to expand my horizons beyond a strict focus on production systems to the far more complicated and less-concrete arena of food policy. I am also endebted to the series editor Mary Helms for the patience she has shown in helping us to pull together the final volume. I have spent a good part of the last fourteen months in Africa. Individual authors have been equally hard to catch within the continental United States.

Jeanne Harlow has had a major role in editing the chapters and performing the myriad tasks that are involved in turning presented papers into polished text.

Finally, I would like to thank the consulting firm Tropical Research and Development for various types of backup support they have accorded to Jeanne and me over the last year. We would also like to thank Jim Seale, Tom Reardon, Michael Cernea, David Brokensha, Ray Hopkins, Paul Doughty, and Art Hansen for their comments and ideas concerning draft chapters and outlines.

Mexico's Two Green Revolutions: Feed for Food

Billie R. DeWalt and David Barkin

Most people would not quarrel with the statement that a truly effective food policy must address the issues of food production, distribution, and consumption (e.g., Gittinger, Leslie, and Hoisington 1987). The successful integration of these three aspects of food policy, however, is rarely accomplished in practice. To demonstrate this point, we consider the case of Mexico, a country that has experienced a political revolution and two Green Revolutions in crop production in this century. The first Green Revolution refers to the dramatic increases in wheat productivity during the 1950s and 1960s; the second to the more recent increases in sorghum production, largely for animal feed, since 1960.[1]

The two Green Revolutions were galvanized by a series of policy interventions by the national government, foreign donors, and transnational corporations. These policies included substantial investment in agronomic research on certain crops, price policies favoring some commodities and discriminating against others, and government subsidies for irrigation, to promote mechanization, and to utilize agricultural inputs (fertilizers and pesticides). The net result of these policies was to stimulate farmers to adopt new crops and new technologies that have substantially increased crop productivity per unit of land.

The benefits of this increased production, however, have not been evenly spread throughout Mexican society. For example, there has not been a parallel increase in the productivity of maize, the basic staple of the vast majority of rural and urban Mexicans. Moreover, the major beneficiaries of the increased productivity of wheat and sorghum have been those rural and urban Mexicans who were already better off before the Green Revolutions. This badly skewed pattern of production and consumption helps explain why, despite significantly greater per capita increases in total production, malnutrition and hunger remain significant problems for low-income rural and urban Mexicans.

The results presented in this chapter are derived from a collaborative project between the University of Kentucky and the Universidad Autónoma Metropolitana—Xochimilco that was funded by the International Sorghum/Millet Collaborative Research Support Program (Reeves, De-Walt, and DeWalt 1987). This project involved both a macrolevel study of the Mexican food system and a microlevel study of farming systems in four villages in various parts of the country. Our research was designed to determine the major factors that have been involved in the evolution of the Mexican food system—production, distribution, and consumption—since 1940.

THE AGRARIAN BACKGROUND

At the beginning of the bloody Revolution (1910) in Mexico, an estimated 800 haciendas controlled approximately 90 percent of the land. Not surprisingly, the slogan *Tierra y Libertad* (land and liberty) was a frequent rallying cry of the revolutionaries. Despite the efforts of the more than one million peasants who died in the Revolution, however, significant land reform did not occur until Lázaro Cárdenas became president of the Republic in 1934. Taking office just after the onset of the Great Depression, Cárdenas was in a position to advocate a path for Mexico that was different from that of urban industrialism. As one of his officials put it in 1935:

> We believe that Mexico finds herself in a privileged position to determine her destiny. . . . By observing the effects of the last crisis of the capitalistic world, we think that we should be able to use the advantages of the industrial era without having to suffer from its well-known shortcomings. . . . We have dreamt of a Mexico of *ejidos* and small industrial communities, electrified, with sanitation, in which goods will be produced for the purpose of satisfying the needs of the people, in which machinery will be employed to relieve man from heavy toil, and not for so-called overproduction. (Beteta 1935:44, quoted in Hewitt de Alcantara 1976:4)

Cárdenas's agrarian socialist dream was materialized in a plan for stimulating agricultural growth by enlarging and strengthening the land reform sector. Consequently, vast land areas were distributed and public expenditures began to flow toward the *ejidos*—the organizations of peasant farmers formed to receive the expropriated lands of the large estates. By 1940, the end of Cárdenas's term as president, 48 percent of the cultivable land had passed into the hands of *ejidos*. Their relatively high productivity is evidenced by the fact that in 1940 they were generating approximately 51 percent of the value of agricultural production (de Janvry 1981:127).

In the early 1940s Mexico experienced a number of changes that affected public policy toward rural agriculture. The election of Manuel Avila Camacho brought to power leaders who did not share the agrarian socialist dream of Cárdenas. Different social priorities became important, and the land reform efforts drastically slowed. At the same time, the wartime disruptions of trade offered Mexican entrepreneurs the opportunity to supply domestic markets with goods that could no longer be procured from foreign markets and to supply foreign markets with goods they had previously purchased from countries now involved in the war effort. A new industrial elite initiated a period of prolonged capitalist growth based on the now familiar pattern of extracting resources from agriculture to industrialize.

THE FIRST GREEN REVOLUTION

It was in this context that the Rockefeller Foundation began discussions in the early 1940s with the Mexican government about the possibility of sponsoring a new research program to contribute to raising agricultural productivity in Mexico by developing new seed varieties. A special unit, the Office of Special Studies (OSS), was created in 1943 within the Ministry of Agriculture to work with the Rockefeller Foundation.[2] The purpose of the OSS "was to increase the production of varieties, the improvement of the soil and the control of insect pests and plant diseases. A corollary goal was to train young men and women in agricultural research and in the development of techniques for promoting the rapid adoption of the new technology" (Wellhausen 1976:128–29). Because maize and wheat together accounted for more than 70 percent of the cultivated land, primary emphasis was placed on those two crops.

At first, the OSS was staffed primarily by Americans, though as the program went on, more and more posts were filled by Mexicans returning from graduate studies in the United States. Eventually, all Mexican agricultural research programs were consolidated into a new, more powerful Instituto Nacional de Investigaciones Agricolas (INIA) in 1961, charged with basic and applied agronomic research in Mexico. At the same time, pure research to extend the initial seed development efforts in wheat and maize were transferred to the *Centro Internacional de Mejoramiento de Maíz y Trigo* (CIMMYT or International Center for the Improvement of Maize and Wheat), established with international funding in 1963.[3]

During the 1940s, when the OSS was just being established, only a few individuals raised questions concerning the directions the program was taking. Two of the criticisms, however, were quite prophetic and merit some discussion.

First, an outstanding cultural geographer of Latin America, Carl Sauer, recommended that agricultural research be directed toward the rural poor. He noted that Mexican small farmers used sound agricultural and nutritional practices and that their main problems were economic rather than agronomic or cultural. Sauer cautioned against the attempt to recreate the model of U.S. commercial agriculture in Mexico:

> A good aggressive bunch of American agronomists and plant breeders could ruin the native resources for good and all by pushing their American commercial stocks. . . . Mexican agriculture cannot be pointed toward standardization on a few commercial types without upsetting native economy and culture hopelessly. The example of Iowa is about the most dangerous of all for Mexico. Unless the Americans understand that, they'd better keep out of this country entirely. This must be approached from an appreciation of native economies as being basically sound. (quoted in Jennings 1988:51)

Influential people in the Rockefeller Foundation dismissed Sauer's warnings as the concerns of someone who thought of Mexico as "a kind of glorified ant hill," more concerned about the destruction of "picturesque folk ways" than "any effort to improve the ants" (Jennings 1988:55).

Further criticism concerned the political, economic, and social effects of new technologies. A report prepared in 1949 by a group led by John Dickey (then President of Dartmouth College) noted: "For example, I can imagine that this program before long might begin to have a considerable impact upon the whole land-use policies of Mexico, and I am perfectly sure that within three to five years the program will raise some very acute problems with respect to the political control of these benefits. . . . These very benefits may introduce fresh economic disparities within the Mexican economy, which will present political problems not now even dimly perceived by many Mexicans" (quoted in Jennings 1988:56). While Dickey recognized potential problems, he avoided any attempt to offer a solution to the possible growth in social tensions: "It would be unfortunate for all concerned, especially for the program itself, if the Foundation is heavily in the picture when this [growth in social tensions] takes place" (quoted in Jennings 1988:57).

A similar posture of avoidance was adopted by the International Agricultural Research Centers in subsequent years. Centers hoped to deflect potential criticisms that might arise concerning the political, economic, and social effects of new technology by indicating that they are only involved in the production of intermediate goods—germ plasm, training, and other expertise—which national programs then use to produce the crop varieties and cultivation technologies that are disseminated to farms within their countries.

The results achieved by the research scientists in the wheat breeding program of the OSS changed the face of world agriculture through what became known as the Green Revolution.

Wheat

The success of the program to increase wheat productivity cannot be disputed. Notably, although the amount of land planted in wheat did not vary significantly from 1940 to 1984 (Figure 1), the production of wheat in Mexico increased from an average of 425,000 tons in 1940–44 to more than 2.7 million tons per year in 1975–79 (Figure 2). Yields during the same time span increased by almost 500 percent averaging approximately 4100 kilograms per hectare (Figure 3). The steady increase in yields resulted in a dramatic turnaround in the country's position in the world market. Mexico imported more than 300,000 tons per year during the early 1950s but exported an average of more than 250,000 tons of wheat per year between 1965 and 1969. Norman Borlaug, director of the OSS wheat experimentation program, received

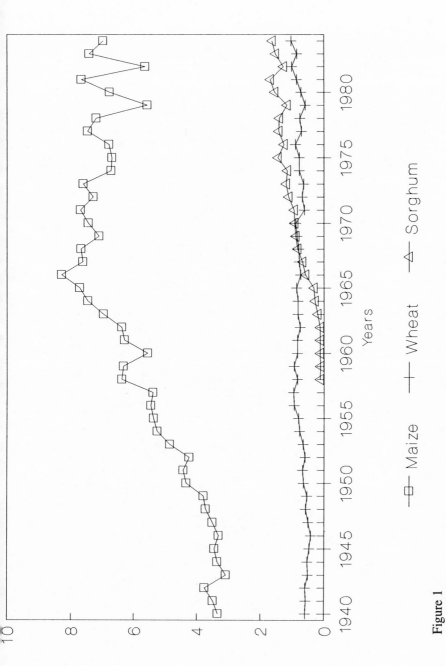

Figure 1

Hectares of Land Sown: Maize, Wheat, and Sorghum, 1940–1984

Sources: DGEA (1981) and INEGI (1987)

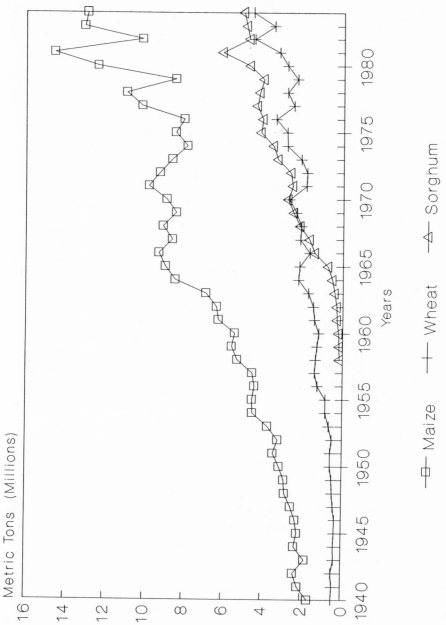

Figure 2
Production of Major Crops: Maize, Wheat, and Sorghum, 1940–1984

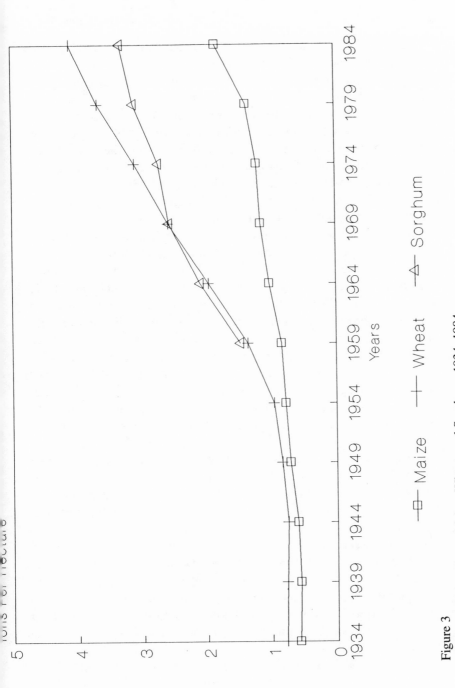

Figure 3
Yields of Major Crops: Maize, Wheat, and Sorghum, 1934–1984
Sources: DGEA (1981) and INEGI (1987)

the Nobel Peace prize in 1970 for his work in creating the miracle seeds that made this rise in productivity possible.

Mexico's experience with wheat shows that the huge increases in yields were made possible by a combination of factors. Two plant-breeding breakthroughs were quite important. The first was the release of semidwarf commercial varieties that had a higher tillering capacity, more grain-filled heads, and shorter stems that made them resistant to lodging. Introduced in the early 1960s, these were the first real varieties to increase the maximum genetic yield potential (Borlaug 1983:690). The second breakthrough was the breeding of varieties generally insensitive to differing day lengths. This made wheat varieties widely adaptable to diverse environments within Mexico and transferable to locations from Canada to Argentina (Borlaug 1983:690).[4]

These miracle seeds, however, were only part of the story. The development of new, high-yielding plant varieties—widely adaptable, responsive to fertilizer, and resistant to disease—was one of three technological factors that together made up the Green Revolution. The others were (1) the development of an improved package of agricultural practices, including better land management, adequate fertilization, and more effective control of weeds and insects, all of which made it possible for the improved varieties to more fully realize their high yield potential; and (2) a favorable ratio between the cost of fertilizer and other inputs and the price the farmer received for his product (Wellhausen 1976:130).

Government investment and subsidization must also be added to the list of factors that created the Green Revolution. The opening up of new irrigated lands, primarily in the northern states of Sonora and Sinaloa, was perhaps the most important explanation for expanded wheat production. Although Sonora and Sinaloa provided only 17 percent of Mexico's wheat production in 1940, by 1964 Sonoran farmers alone produced 71 percent of total production (Hewitt de Alcantara 1976:167). Mexico invested heavily in irrigation as a means of expanding agricultural production; between 1940 and 1980 at least 80 percent of total federal expenditures on agriculture went for construction of irrigation facilities or programs associated with these works (Barkin and Suárez 1986:104).

In addition, the Mexican government poured millions of pesos into constructing roads and railroads for crop transportation, constructing storage facilities, establishing crop insurance programs, rendering considerable assistance to small and large farmers to mechanize their operations, and providing substantial credit to modernize production of wheat. However, in spite of all of these government inputs for infrastructure, wheat production in Mexico did not begin substantially increasing until the government established a guaranteed price for wheat of 913 pesos per ton, a price that was in effect from 1954 until 1964 (Hewitt de Alcantara 1976:90, 309). This price was substantially above the world market price for the grain; consequently, Mexico's wheat exports during the period constituted a net loss in revenue to the government. Government guaranteed prices for wheat amounted to a subsidy to wheat growers of about 250 million pesos per year (20 million dollars) (Hewitt de Alcantara 1976:308–39).

Thus, the impressive improvement in wheat production and Mexico's emergence during the 1960s as an exporter of wheat must be recognized as not simply the triumph of technology that created miracle seeds but also as substantial government investment and subsidization of infrastructure, fertilizer, storage, crop insurance, credit, and irrigation. These services were theoretically available to all agriculturalists, but in fact they were accessible primarily to the best-endowed, politically powerful farming groups in newly opened regions. The smallholders in Central Mexico who had produced most of the country's wheat in the past were generally unable to compete with the high productivity levels prevailing in the northwestern states of Sinaloa and Sonora.

Despite continuing increases in average yields, the first Green Revolution in Mexico has been stagnating (Figure 3). Since the price subsidies for wheat were removed after 1964 and its price relative to maize steadily eroded (Yates 1981), the amount of land planted in wheat declined (Figure 1). Prior to the 1980s, despite the continuing increase in yields, only in 1976 (when more than 894,000 hectares were reported under cultivation) did the amount of land planted in wheat approximate that of the decade between 1955 and 1964. Real prices of wheat during the late 1970s did not approach those prevailing in the period between 1953 and 1971 (Dirección General de Economía Agrícola [DGEA] January 1980:29), and commercial farmers converted their operations to more profitable crops such as vineyards, chick-peas, sorghum, and safflower. By 1979, approximately 588,341 hectares were planted in wheat.

Demand for wheat in Mexico has continued to increase at a relatively moderate pace. As has happened in many other parts of the developing world, consumer preferences have increasingly shifted away from traditional diet staples such as the *tortilla* to wheat products such as bread, cookies, crackers, and cakes. While this tendency is most pronounced in urban areas, *bolillos* (a roll much like French bread), *Pan Bimbo* (a popular packaged bread), *Donas* (packaged donuts), *Tuinkys* (Twinkies), and many other such products are now common items in rural communities where they are consumed primarily by the more affluent families (DeWalt 1981, 1983a). The industries that produce these wheat products are marked by a high degree of concentration, with a few large mills producing the bulk of the production. The harder Green Revolution wheats required new milling technology. Many smaller mills were forced to close because they were unable to afford the new inputs to handle the harder wheat varieties (Barkin and Suárez 1986:134).

Because of the relative stagnation of wheat production since 1965, combined with continuing demand, Mexico resorted to importing the commodity. Net imports have averaged more than 500,000 tons per year since 1970, climbing to more than one million tons, more than one-third of the country's needs, in each year from 1979 to 1981.

By 1985 wheat imports disappeared once again as a result of sizable increases in the guaranteed price and administrative decisions to oblige farmers in the irrigated districts to plant a certain proportion of their land in wheat to obtain irrigation permits for other, more lucrative crops. In both 1982 and 1984, more than 1 million hectares were planted in wheat. The government found that national self-sufficiency in wheat could be achieved relatively easily through direct intervention because the wheat farmers are so highly concentrated in a few regions of the country and because they are so dependent on government-subsidized irrigation water. Although the Green Revolution greatly increased the productivity of land planted in wheat, policy measures unpopular with the farmers themselves have been required to assure sufficient production.

Maize

The second major crop in which the OSS and its successors were interested was maize. Compared to the success of the wheat program, maize production has been a comparative failure. Maize yields per hectare have approximately doubled since 1940, but they are still not very impressive in terms of their rate of increase when compared with yields in other countries or with other grain crops in Mexico (especially sorghum and wheat). As of 1984, yields were only approximately 1.83 tons per hectare (Figure 3).

The amount of land planted in maize has also not increased or even approximated that of the mid-1960s; in 1984 it was less than 7 million hectares. Maize production has continued to increase because of some improvement in yields but has not kept up with demand in the country (Figure 2). In order to provide for existing demand for this basic grain in the face of a stagnation in production, Mexico has imported substantial quantities of maize—an average of more than 1,100,000 tons per year during the 1970s (more than one-eighth of national production) and substantially larger quantities in the 1980s.

The failure to achieve higher levels of maize yields has been especially disappointing for reasons other than the necessity to import grain. Mexico is probably the area of the world in which maize was first domesticated, yet the country's average yields of the crop are far below those of many other countries. For example, U.S. maize yields average almost three times those of wheat per hectare (Borlaug 1983:691), while Mexico's wheat yields average three times those of maize. In addition, maize is generally acknowledged to have a higher maximum genetic yield potential than the other cereals (Borlaug 1983:692). Why then have the attempts to raise maize yields in Mexico not met with success?

The principal factor identified as impeding the improvement of Mexico's maize production is that maize is produced primarily under rainfed conditions by hundreds of thousands of subsistence farmers. Census figures from 1960 indicated that while maize farmers possessed an average of only 3 hectares each with only 9.5 percent of maize land irrigated, the average size of wheat farms was 17 hectares with 70 percent of this land irrigated (Hewitt de Alcantara 1976:24). Maize farmers with small holdings and without access to irrigation facilities were unlikely to have the resources to afford fertilizers, insecticides, and herbicides. As we have seen in an examination of wheat production, the high yield potential of improved varieties is best achieved when used in combination with a package of modern agricultural practices and inputs. Average production figures for maize are lowered substantially by poor yields achieved on the small plots of *ejidatarios* and other small-scale farmers. Yet if maize yields and profits were high enough, commercial farmers would produce maize rather than wheat, sorghum, or other crops. For example, during 1980–82, when maize prices were raised, farmers substantially increased the amount of land planted in maize (*see also* Austin and Esteva 1987).

There are several interdependent reasons why commercial farmers are not interested in producing maize. A major factor is that the maize-breeding programs of the OSS, INIA, and CIMMYT have yet to release open-pollinated varieties or hybrids that can compete with those of wheat or sorghum. In fact, research has shown that good smallholder selection procedures consistently produce higher yielding seeds than the research stations can offer on the marketplace for dryland cultivation (Felstehausen and Diaz-Cisneros 1985). Even hybrid maize seeds offer little advantage. In 1970, for example, the average yields with hybrids were only slightly more than 70 percent of the average of all wheat yields. In our conversations with farmers in the Bajío, one of Mexico's richest agricultural areas, we were told that yields of wheat and sorghum are consistently above those of maize even on lands of the best farmers.

Mexican and CIMMYT maize breeders claim that the results of their breeding work are substantial and that the primary reason why maize yields in Mexico are so low is that the improved seeds have not been distributed effectively to farmers. These protestations are not without some validity. The Maize Commission, formed in the late 1940s to multiply and distribute improved seed, was rendered ineffective and inefficient by its political rivalry with the OSS, which restricted funding. Since 1961, the responsibility for the production of high yielding seeds of all types has been in the hands of the Productora Nacional de Semillas (PRONASE). The seeds produced by PRONASE have been of low quality, while administrative costs have been high and their system of distribution unreliable (Hewitt de Alcantara 1976:77; Barkin and Suárez 1983). In contrast, the maize seeds produced under contract by private farmers for private multinational seed companies are highly regarded and sold to those producing yellow maize for animal feed; they also distribute the majority of the hybrid sorghum seeds (see below). As a consequence, less than 20 percent of the maize crop is sown with improved seed while the proportion of wheat and sorghum produced with improved seed is more than 90 percent.

The final factor that may contribute to the disinterest of commercial farmers for maize relates to its marketability—maize is not as amenable to marketing to a few large private consumers. While wheat and sorghum can be sold in large quantities to manufacturers that process the grain, maize is utilized in millions of homes and thousands of *tortillerias* (enterprises that market machine-made tortillas). More importantly, because maize is so important as a basis of the subsistence system, the government has tried to keep prices down. Consequently, the real price for maize has remained relatively constant at a time when the real prices for many other crops have been increasing (Yates 1981:218). Many farmers have shifted their commercial production to these other crops—which are produced primarily for animal feeds, upper-income Mexican consumers (Barkin 1982; Barkin and DeWalt 1988; DeWalt 1985b, 1988), and export (Feder 1977)—retaining the cultivation of maize only for household consumption needs.

Thus, the majority of the national production of maize has remained in the hands of small subsistence farmers cultivating rainfed plots without resources to purchase inputs. Even those farmers who had more resources than average have had little incentive to grow corn. For example, some farmers in the central highlands who had irrigated land and received credit for fertilizer were producing an average of 1569 kilograms per hectare in 1973 (DeWalt 1979:282). Although this was better than the average national yields, with an average of only 2.38 hectares and deducting the cost of inputs, even good farmers made a profit of only U.S. $300 per year (DeWalt and DeWalt 1980:307–11). Under such conditions it is not surprising that these farmers said that *maíz no es negocio* (maize is not business) and were primarily interested in this crop only for household consumption, not for sale.

The combination of more productive alternatives to maize, whether because the seeds are inherently more productive or because PRONASE cannot produce enough good quality seed to meet the needs, and more profitable alternatives to maize means that not enough of this crop is being produced domestically to meet the demand. Thus, Mexico imports enormous quantities of maize, reaching a high of 4.6 million tons in 1983. The imported yellow maize available on the world market is generally produced for animal consumption. It is a poor substitute for the domestic white maize preferred for making tortillas; many consumers complain about the cardboard texture and the inferior taste of the tortillas made with yellow maize.

Two of the main architects of the OSS and CIMMYT have recently admitted that, in retrospect, much more attention should have been paid to the breeding of varieties of maize that would meet the needs of the resource-poor, small farmers who grow the crop in rainfed areas (Wellhausen 1976:150; Borlaug 1983:691). In recent years CIMMYT has been devoting considerable efforts to the breeding of better varietal populations assuming that this has greater potential for increasing yields among small farmers because these people are less likely to be able to use the hybrids. As articulated by Yates, "The farmers most receptive to technology have already modernized their practices, and those that remain to be approached are deeply traditionalist" (1981:138).

National program and CIMMYT technologists remain unmoved by research among small farmers that has demonstrated the superiority of alternative approaches. On numerous occasions, Mexican agronomists have found that the yield potential of open-pollinated varieties developed through inherited selection procedures are superior to those available from genetic modification programs for the dryland conditions prevalent in many smallholder settings in Mexico. More than twenty years of experimentation and intervention by the National Agricultural College of Chapingo (Felstehausen and Diaz-Cisneros 1985) demonstrated that, for small-scale producers, economics as well as technology have led to the massive abandonment of maize cultivation. They simply cannot make enough money growing maize to justify farming.

The efforts of the OSS and its successors are important because they represent one of the first attempts to systematically apply the scientific method in agricultural research to the solution of problems in the food grain sector of developing countries. Previously such attention had been devoted exclusively to export crops. These efforts were only part of the explanation for the transformation of the agricultural sector in Mexico. Other events and processes were under way as well.

TRANSFORMATION OF THE AGRICULTURAL
SECTOR IN MEXICO

While much of the world's attention was focused on the Green Revolution success of wheat, Mexican agriculture was undergoing other profound changes: (1) a substantial increase in the area cultivated in the country, and (2) a marked change in the composition of cultigens grown on this expanded area (for example, Barkin 1982; Centro de Estudios de Planeación Agropecuaria [CESPA] 1982; Rama and Rello 1982; Barkin and Suárez 1986).[5]

An important factor in explaining the growth in cultivated area in the country was the increasing availability of irrigation. Government policy since the 1940s has favored the construction of large irrigation districts in zones previously not amenable to cultivation. River basin development commissions were organized during the presidency of Miguel Aleman (1946–52) to expand production frontiers as a strategy for stimulating agriculture (Barkin and King 1970). Between 1940 and 1979, irrigation constituted between 70 percent and 99.2 percent of the total budget invested in the agricultural sector (Sanderson 1984:118; Barkin and Suárez 1986). The result of this policy has been a significant increase in the proportion of the nation's irrigated area—from less than 14 percent in 1950 to more than 22 percent a quarter of a century later and as much as one quarter of the cultivated area currently (DGEA 1983a:21). Although these figures probably overestimate the real irrigated area, Mexico is one of the countries with the highest proportion of irrigated to total cultivated land in the world.

Since 1940 the amount of cultivated land has expanded at a rate of more than 2.4 percent annually. The area cultivated increased more than 2.5 times while the area opened to irrigation increased to more than 3 times the area of 1940 (Barkin and DeWalt 1988:32). Mexican agricultural output would thus have experienced a substantial increase even without the improvements in yields generated by the Green Revolution and the substantial increases in use of fertilizer.

The crops grown on this increased agricultural base have also changed substantially. Government policy during the 1930s and 1940s stressed increasing domestic food production. National programs like the agrarian reform and irrigation development were originally defended by policymakers as strategies to raise food production.

After World War II, however, the expansion of national and international markets for agricultural products led to shifts in the strategies of the more commercially oriented farmers. With the assistance of government policy and subsidies, commercial farmers began making major changes in technology, opting for more capital-intensive production technology using fertilizers, pesticides, improved seeds, mechaniza-

Fruits and vegetables at market, Choluteca, Honduras. Photograph by
B. DeWalt.

tion, and other practices to increase productivity and profitability. For
example, at the end of the 1970s the use of fertilizers was growing
at an annual rate of approximately 13 percent per year, and between
1940 and 1980 the number of tractors in the country grew at a rate of
more than 9 percent per year (DGEA 1983a:27, 1983b). The increasing availability of government agricultural credit lowered the cost of
these and other inputs and facilitated the expansion of the physical productivity of the land for wealthier farmers. This trend toward capital-
intensive production methods, however, caused significant changes in
the use of labor; permanent employees were replaced by machinery
and by temporary and migratory laborers, and the results were social
and economic dislocations. While employment in the rural modern sector expanded from 31.7 percent of the total employed in agriculture in
1950 to 51 percent in 1980, the number of self-employed agricultural
workers actually decreased (Couriel 1984:56).

In addition, the area cultivated with fruits and vegetables has expanded significantly, a process stimulated by agroindustrial investment
(Feder 1977; Rama and Vigorito 1979). At the same time, in certain

parts of the public administrative apparatus, there was a greater concern for the rational and profitable commercial production of products like cotton, coffee, and tobacco. Expansion in these cash crops for the world market has thus been stimulated both by the efforts of government policymakers as well as the efforts of private producers.

Most important, the modernization of Mexican agriculture since 1965 has been characterized by phenomenal growth of the livestock sector. Production of pigs, chickens, and cattle has been booming (Barkin and DeWalt 1988:34). Per capita consumption of eggs doubled in the last forty years, poultry production trebled in the past thirty years to 150 million birds, and hog production grew almost as rapidly to 12.8 million head in 1980 (Yates 1981:103–5; USDA 1981:7). This expansion in the livestock sector has taken place through a modernization process that has increasingly "industrialized" production. This process has substituted technological systems that rely on cultivated pastures, improved breeds of animals, heavy use of antibiotics, and confined feeding of industrially-produced balanced animal feeds for natural pastures, household wastes, and other similar resources that had been used for household production of livestock. The result is that land utilization has been changing rapidly; the fastest growing sectors of Mexican agriculture have been in the production of feed grains and oilseeds.

THE SECOND GREEN REVOLUTION: SORGHUM

The most striking example of this shift toward production of feed grains in Mexico is provided by the expansion of sorghum cultivation and use. Sorghum was unknown in the traditional agriculture of Mexico. Except for a few exceptional, unsuccessful experiments during the first half of the century, it was not cultivated systematically. In 1944, however, foreign agronomists from the OSS began experimental work with sorghum. Their work began with the premise that drought-tolerant sorghum might help to resolve the problems of areas marginal for maize, those in which rainfall was either limited or poorly distributed (Pitner, de la Vega, and Durón 1954:1).

Early experiments did not meet with great success nor with much interest among agriculturalists. It was only at the end of the 1950s that great interest in the grain was shown. In 1957, the Rockefeller Foundation annual report on the Mexican Agricultural Program reported, "Interest in sorghums has grown considerably during the last year principally because of the rapid expansion of the livestock industry, especially pork and poultry production. As a result of recent heavy demand, the price of sorghum grain in Mexico City has increased from $400–450 pesos a metric ton at harvest time in 1955 to $790 pesos in May, 1957" (Rockefeller Foundation 1957:77).

Since 1958, when the government began collecting statistics on sorghum, the crop's history is nothing short of spectacular (Figures 1 and 2). During the period 1965–80, when the area cultivated in the country was growing at a rate of 1.5 percent per year, area cultivated in sorghum was growing at a rate of 13 percent per year. By 1984, sorghum occupied more than 1.5 million hectares—one-fourth the area of maize and more than twice the area of wheat, the miracle crop of the first Green Revolution. In terms of the amount produced, sorghum's growth was even more rapid—18 percent per year. Today sorghum occupies the second largest area sown in Mexico, but despite Mexico's having become the fifth largest producer in the world, the amount produced is not sufficient to satisfy increasing demand. In some recent years, the country has had to import 50 percent of the national production, making the country the second largest importer of sorghum from the United States.

The reasons for the second Green Revolution in sorghum involve a combination of technological and ecological, as well as socioeconomic, factors (DeWalt 1985b). From the technological point of view, the production of sorghum in Mexico benefited from the creation of sorghum hybrids developed in Texas. Until 1955, large-scale production of sorghum hybrids was not possible. With the discovery of male sterile plants, however, sorghum hybrid production increased so rapidly that by 1960 approximately 95 percent of the sorghum in the United States was sown with hybrid seed (Quinby 1971:17–19). Mexican farmers quickly recognized the productivity of U.S. hybrids and began replacing maize with sorghum or introducing it into newly opened areas. Thus, widely adaptable and highly productive hybrid sorghums from the United States were quickly adopted by Mexican farmers *without* the benefit of national or international government programs to encourage production, *without* the sponsorship of any bilateral or multilateral aid agency, and *without* the teaching and technical assistance of any extension agents.

At the same time, transnational animal feed companies were transforming poultry- and pig-raising technology and creating a burgeoning demand for sorghum. In 1964, for example, Ralston-Purina began a campaign promoting the benefits of sorghum, discussing the cultural practices necessary to grow it, and providing hybrid seed from the United States to producers. Finally, the company offered to buy, at an attractive price, all of the sorghum being produced—for use in its diverse lines of nutritionally balanced livestock feeds.

Because of the importance of maize in the national food system, Mexico would not allow private seed companies to compete with the Maize Commission and its successor in producing and selling improved maize varieties and hybrids. Laws regulating the transnational seed companies like DeKalb, Pioneer, Northrup-King, Asgrow, and Funk existed for maize, but no such laws for sorghum were in effect (Barkin and Suárez 1983:102–107). Thus, transnational companies responded quickly to the demand for hybrid sorghum seed by establishing research and marketing operations in Mexico. The marketed hybrids are basically the same high-yielding seeds bred for use as animal feed in the United States. Because virtually all of the sorghum in Mexico is planted using hybrid seed (Barkin and Suárez 1983), its adoption and use must surely qualify as one of the most successful cases of diffusion of innovation of all time (Rogers 1971).

Yields of sorghum in Mexico have been much higher than those of maize and reach nearly the average yield of wheat (Figure 3). Under similar technological circumstances on irrigated land, average yields of sorghum were 40 percent higher than those of maize. On rainfed lands, average yields of sorghum were 89 percent higher (Aburto 1979:145). Because agricultural scientists agree that maize has higher yield potential, the poor performance of maize must be attributed to the failure of the national agricultural research and seed system to deliver a competitive variety or hybrid. These deficiencies are compounded by the relative lack of credit and the disadvantageous producer prices fixed for maize as compared to those prevailing in the much less-regulated domestic market for sorghum.

In addition to the use of hybrid seed, the success of sorghum production has benefited from infrastructural improvements. Although the OSS originally experimented with sorghum for marginal lands, in 1979 more than 36 percent of the sorghum was grown under irrigated conditions. Large extensions of land in such productive irrigated zones as Tamaulipas, Sinaloa, and the Bajío (a highly productive area of central Mexico) are now planted in sorghum, in part because sorghum requires less water than maize or wheat for successful cultivation. In some regions of the country, like the Bajío, that have experienced droughts in recent years, the government has sometimes had to limit irrigation water because the reservoirs have been at low levels. Bajío farmers in 1982, for example, were allowed to irrigate only twice rather than four times as had been their practice. Under such conditions, sorghum has a definite advantage.

Sorghum has also benefited from the Mexican government's policies to encourage mechanization and the use of agricultural inputs. The cultivation of sorghum is highly mechanized; tractors are used for plowing, seeding, and cultivating and combines are used for harvesting. Sorghum has thus benefited from the heavy subsidies accorded tractor production, operation, and purchase (Yates 1981:129). Even *ejidatarios* interviewed in the Bajío, San Luis Potosí, Sinaloa, Michoacan, and Morelos use manual labor only in some hand weeding and in scaring away birds just before the harvest. All other operations are carried out by rented tractors and combines. Hired trucks work in concert with the combines to carry the grain immediately to the granaries of the companies manufacturing balanced livestock feeds.

Sorghum has come to be seen by the farmer as a crop with many advantages compared with the relatively more labor-intensive maize, which requires between two and ten times as many person/days of labor per hectare. Sorghum is also a less risky undertaking because it is more drought-tolerant than other crops. In addition, farmers report that there is little need to worry about "midnight harvests" of sorghum. In some areas, a substantial amount of the maize is stolen by passersby; in contrast there is no such risk for sorghum because it is not grown for human consumption in Mexico. The high degree of mechanization is attractive to the smaller farmers who have off-farm employment (Roberts 1982; 1985). In one community in San Luis Potosí, for example, more than 50 percent of ejidatarios had been to the United States as illegal migrants within the past five years. These individuals continue as part-time farmers because very little of their own labor is required, allowing them to seek more remunerative work in other places (DeWalt and Barkin 1987).

The government price support system has also contributed significantly to making sorghum an attractive crop. The most rapid increases in sorghum production came in the mid-1960s. In fact, sorghum production nearly doubled from 747,000 tons in 1965 to more than 1.4 million tons in 1966, while basic foodgrain production stagnated (Figure 1). This critical turning point in Mexican agriculture saw the confluence of two important government policy changes. First, as a result of the cost of the program, the government decided to freeze price supports for most grains in 1964; the guaranteed price for wheat was actually dropped from 913 pesos to 800 pesos per ton. The second important policy change was the initiation of a guaranteed price of 625 pesos per ton for sorghum in 1965. The effects of these two actions made wheat and maize less attractive crops than they had been previously and made sorghum more attractive. Many farmers who had previously grown wheat switched to sorghum or to other higher-value cash crops (Hewitt de Alcantara 1976). A similar pattern emerged on a much larger scale among maize farmers.

The price of sorghum has been between 58 percent and 84 percent of the price of maize during the last two decades (DGEA 1982). With its higher yields, lower input costs, and reduced risk, sorghum is still a more attractive crop than maize, even at these lower prices.

The final element that has contributed to the growth of sorghum in Mexico has been the steadily increasing demand for the product, a demand that comes exclusively from the animal feed industry. Between 1950 and 1975, the number of establishments producing animal feed grew from 19 to more than 305. Since then the number has grown explosively as new firms and farmers themselves compete to produce the relatively standardized product. While production is distributed nearly equally between national and transnational corporations, a few transnational corporations like Ralston-Purina and Anderson-Clayton virtually control key ingredients in this industry (Barkin and Suárez 1980: 135–36).

As indicated earlier, industrialized production of eggs, poultry, and hogs is the most dynamic sector in rural Mexico. Although the animal feed industry also uses maize, barley, wheat bran, soybeans, and other products, sorghum supplies 74 percent of the raw material used in animal feed in Mexico (Boletin Interno 1982a, 1982b, 1982c). The expansion of sorghum production, the emergence of the specialized feed industry, and the growth of poultry and hog production have gone hand in hand. The existence and growth of each industry makes possible the expansion of the other.

Despite the phenomenal growth of sorghum production, the country is still unable to grow enough to satisfy demand. In 1983, the country imported 3.3 million tons of sorghum, approximately 40 percent of the total utilized. Sorghum thus epitomizes the trends in Mexican agriculture toward what Barkin (1982) has called *ganaderización* (livestock-oriented production). That is, a growing share of rural resources is devoted to fodder production for livestock to provide an affluent diet for wealthy and middle-class Mexicans whose income increased substantially during the 1970s (*see* Hardy 1982), making possible an increase in their demand for sources of animal protein.

THE RESULTS OF MEXICO'S TWO GREEN REVOLUTIONS

The result of the technological changes that occurred in Mexican agriculture is that by 1980 grain production in Mexico had increased approximately eight times what it was in 1940, a time period in which the population only trebled (DeWalt 1985b:44–45). Annual availability of the major grains in Mexico in 1984 was more than 500 kilograms per capita (Figure 4). Per capita domestic production of grains was more than 300 kilograms per year, a figure that is more than double the 131 kilograms of 1940 (B. DeWalt 1985b:50). Given these data, one would have predicted in 1940 that Mexico would have solved its food availability problems.

Such is not the case, however. The problem is that food grains are being replaced by feed grains. Animals have increasingly been inserted in the middle of the food chain between grains and people. Land use patterns in Mexico have been changing even more rapidly than Dickey and others associated with OSS might have expected; the fastest growing sectors of Mexican agriculture have been in the production of feed grains and oilseeds.

Enormous quantities of natural resources are now devoted to the pro-

Per Capita

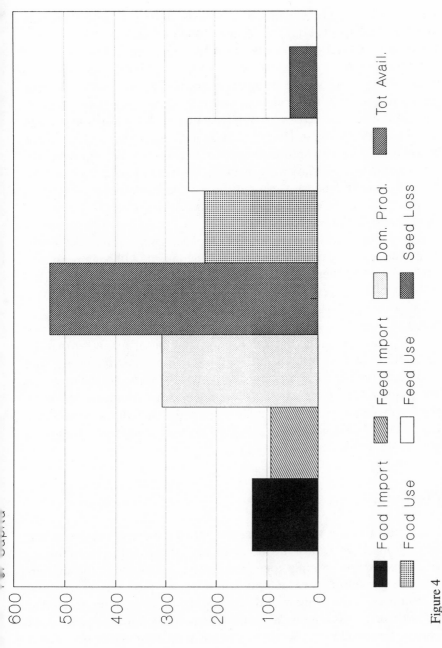

600

500

400

300

200

100

0

Food Import   Feed Import   Dom. Prod.   Tot Avail.

Food Use   Feed Use   Seed Loss

Figure 4
Mexican Grains: Sources and Uses, 1984

duction of meat. The proportion of cropland devoted to animal production has gone from about 5 percent in 1960 to more than 23 percent in
1980 (Barkin 1982:66–67), and it has been reported that 64 percent of
the national territory is used to produce only 3,140,000 tons of meat, a
yield of only 24 kilograms per hectare used (García Sordo 1985:8). The
proportion of grain fed to animals has risen steadily, estimated at 6 percent in 1960 (Meissner 1981), 32 percent in 1980 (DeWalt 1985b), and
as high as 48 percent in 1985 (*UnoMásUno* January 10, 1985:1). Large
amounts of domestic production and imports are needed to provide the
approximately 250 kilograms of grain per capita that are needed for
feed (Figure 4). The Mexican nutritionist Chavez has likened this use
of resources to the miracle that Christ performed with the loaves and
the fishes—but in reverse (1982:9).

The social benefits of the use of cropland, grains, and the 74 million hectares of pasture are very poorly distributed. Although per capita
consumption of meat is approximately 42 kilograms per year (DGEA
1982:16), the government itself reported that more than 25 million
Mexicans (more than 35 percent of the population) *never eat meat* and
that less than 30 million drink milk regularly.[6] Although many occasionally consume animal products (eggs and milk), it is clear that the
distribution of the products is sharply skewed towards the upper- and
middle-income groups. Malnutrition is widely accepted to be one of
the country's gravest public health problems; one authoritative source
reports that approximately 40 million (more than half of the population)
are seriously undernourished (UNAM/INN study cited in 8/18/84 issue
of *UnoMásUno*).

CONCLUSIONS

To return to the theme of this chapter, it should be apparent that
effective food policy must link or integrate issues of supply, distribution,
and consumption. Simply focusing on the *supply* of food through increasing agricultural productivity will not solve problems of nutrition
in countries of the Third World. The successful integration of the distribution and consumption aspects of food policy with the production
aspect, however, is rarely accomplished in practice. Instead, modern
agricultural science and much development policy assume that by ad-

dressing the issue of *supply* that the problems of hunger and malnutrition will be solved. The case study of Mexico illustrates how solving the supply problem through large increases in agricultural productivity does not necessarily result in major improvements in access to food for the majority of the population.

The efforts of foreign donors, the national government, and transnational corporations have been notably successful in some areas. The country's farmers have produced ever larger quantities of grain as a result of the two Green Revolutions, but because middle- and upper-class consumers continually demand more luxury food items like meat and dairy products, more and more of the grain is fed to livestock. Poor people have become increasingly marginalized from the food system as is indicated by the continuing high prevalence of under-nutrition in the country.

The overall food system seems to be on a treadmill. As the continuing substitution of food grains for feed grains continues, the national food system of Mexico seems launched on a trajectory in which animal feed is displacing food grains without any thought for the long-term consequences for sustainable economic growth or for political stability.

The trends we have documented for Mexico are occurring in other areas of the developing world as well. The substitution of feed crops for food crops is a dominant trend in worldwide agriculture and, as in Mexico, is usually accompanied by an increasing polarization in the food system. On the one hand, commercially-oriented large farmers receive government assistance and subsidies to produce crops for the increasingly affluent diets of middle- and high-income people. On the other, small farmers face an increasingly hostile economic environment in which to produce basic grains and they, along with the urban and rural poor, have a more and more difficult time getting access to an adequate diet (Barkin, Batt, and DeWalt 1990).

It should be apparent that increasing food supplies through the modernization of agricultural technology will not solve nutrition problems in developing countries. Government and donor agency policies need to be redirected to focus on the kinds of commodities that are produced and, more importantly, on the kinds of producers who will produce them. More availability will not mean much to rural and urban poor who cannot afford to purchase the food. We advocate two major changes in policy that can help alleviate the crisis in the Mexican food system.

First, government policies and subsidies should be redirected. During the period we have considered here, government subsidies differentially benefited larger farmers; producers of fruits, vegetables, and feed crops; farmers with access to irrigation; and livestock producers. Keeping staple food prices low has removed incentives for farmers to produce these crops. Improving the price structure for staple crops like maize and beans, even if this requires subsidization of these crops, would help stimulate the small farm sector and improve these farmers' access to food (see Barkin and DeWalt 1988:49–51 for further elaboration of these points).

Second, the national and international agricultural research system should give greater attention to providing assistance for small farmers who cultivate resource-poor, rainfed areas. The research "subsidies" that government and donor agencies have provided for larger farmers who cultivate the best lands need to be redirected. We believe that these latter farmers will continue to profit from the research of private seed and chemical corporations that will create technology to sell to them. Public and international agency assistance should attempt to mitigate the distributional effects (i.e., larger farmers forcing small farms out of business) that are inherent in the capitalist system.

The bottom line is that much more attention needs to be paid to policies and research to solve food and nutrition problems rather than to increasing productivity. The latter is a relatively simple technological problem while the former involves political and economic choices. Unless these difficult political and economic choices are made, a substantial portion of the population, as in Mexico, will be condemned to poverty and poor nutrition.

NOTES

1. Portions of the information and data in this paper have previously appeared in several other reports of our research (DeWalt 1985b, 1988; DeWalt and Barkin 1987; Barkin and DeWalt 1988). Much has been written, pro and con, about the Green Revolution (see Griffin 1974; Wade 1974; Pearse 1980; Pinstrup-Andersen and Hazell 1987 for contrasting views); we see no need to repeat those arguments here.

2. To many Mexican agronomists, the Rockefeller initiative appeared to be a direct attack on their long-established programs to improve working condi-

tions in small holder areas. Thus, the Mexican group tried to maintain its own separate institutional and programmatic identity (Barkin and Suárez 1983:96). As the political shift in priorities (to give more attention to industrialization and less attention to land reform and the ejido sector) consolidated, the Mexican group of researchers (known as the Instituto de Investigaciones Agricolas and other names) who had tried to retain their own research program were eclipsed by the foreign dominated program.

3. The OSS marked the beginning of the attempts to apply the research breakthroughs made in U.S. and other western agriculture to developing parts of the world, thereby establishing the precedent for creating the system of international agricultural research centers (Plucknett and Smith 1982).

4. It was this characteristic that eventually allowed Mexican wheats to be adapted and grown successfully in such locations as India and Pakistan.

5. There is an abundant literature on the Mexican experience in rural development. Only the main outlines are sketched here.

6. These data are quite difficult to believe. Our experience in rural Mexico suggests that most people occasionally consume meat and other livestock products. These figures should be taken to indicate the severity of the problem of many Mexicans in getting access to meat.

Learning from Experience: Implementing Farming Systems Research and Extension in the Malawi Agricultural Research Project

Art Hansen

Farming Systems Research and Extension (FSR/E), although not always easy to define, is important to effective food policy. Food policies—which attempt to influence the decisionmaking environment of producers, distributors, and consumers—are made in urban offices, but most production decisions in African countries are made in smallholder households, villages, and fields. To be effective, any production component of food policies must grow out of understanding the actual decisionmaking environments affecting farmers. Planners and researchers have much to learn about the technical and socioeconomic environments of these smallholders and the empirical worth of technical recommendations once implemented by farmers under their particular conditions.

This chapter defines the concept and methodology of FSR/E, provides a case example of the approach being implemented in Malawi, and discusses some of the valuable lessons learned from the study. In addition to recognizing the need to learn from the smallholders' experience, as well as our own, the Malawi study revealed:

- the extent of the technical and socioeconomic research necessary to understanding the environment within which African smallholders operate,
- how FSR/E addresses these problems, and
- an awareness of the practical problems involved in implementing any international assistance program.

FARMING SYSTEMS RESEARCH AND EXTENSION

Concepts

Farming Systems Research and Extension is primarily carried out on smallholder farms. The focus of research and the central concept of this approach is the "farming system." While this concept has various definitions (Fresco and Poats 1986; Fresco 1984; Shaner, Philipp, and Schmehl 1982; Norman, Simmons, and Hays 1982), perhaps the one best suited to this discussion is that a farming system is not simply a collection of crops and/or animals to which one can apply an input and expect immediate results but is a complicated interwoven mesh of resources and factors (agronomic, economic, social, cultural, physical, etc.) that are managed to a greater or lesser extent by a farmer. Utilizing the technology he or she knows, this person or family unit attempts to increase or maximize the farmer's or farm household's utility within a given context of accepted preferences, aspirations, and socioeconomic conditions. The farmer's unique understanding and interpretation of the immediate environment, both natural and socioeconomic, is instrumental in creating the farming system (Hansen, Mwango, and Phiri 1982).

The term *utility* refers to a broad range of satisfactions. For Malawi's small farmers, utility definitely includes the provision of foodstuffs, both for the staple dish (*nsima*) and accompanying side dishes (*ndiwo*), as well as the provision of some cash from the sale of crops and/or animals.

Each farmer interprets the opportunities and constraints of the ecological (climate, soils, crops, animals, pests, and plagues) and social (prices, markets, political policies, cultural values, and uses for labor) environment in which he or she lives. Moreover, each farmer then uses available resources to produce a mix of crops and/or animals. The farming system that results is the interaction of environment and resource allocation, integrated by the farmer's management decisions and work. Environmental variables (rainfall, pests, input availability, etc.) may determine whether the farming system successfully satisfies the farmer's desires, but the form of the system itself is determined by the farmer's attempts to cope with anticipated environmental conditions. For example, in areas where droughts are common, farmers anticipate them by including sorghum, millet, and cassava into their farming systems or by early or dry planting.

At one level each farm may be considered a unique farming system. At a more general or abstract level, farms and farmers with similar constraints and opportunities can be grouped into fairly homogeneous categories. The farming systems research program in Malawi (and other programs worldwide) works with categories of systems rather than individual farms because there are not enough research resources to work with individual farms and farmers.

The FSR/E program must first identify the important categories of farming systems in a given geographical area, learn how farms in each category operate (resources, constraints, goals, and relationships), and devise and test alternative technological possibilities that will permit farmers to improve their productivity and utility. The central concept in FSR/E—the farming system—is a complex one that includes many variables because the management decisions that Malawi's smallholders make are complex decisions, and the resulting systems are complex. Almost every decision involves satisfying some goals at the expense of others; almost every action involves weighing relative costs and benefits since available resources have a variety of uses, and applying resources to one activity means they cannot be applied to another.

Farming decisions can be seen as compromises; the farmer continues to balance everything he or she wishes to accomplish against available resources and time. Generally the farmer must cut back on the optimum production practices (in terms of optimizing yield) for each specific crop or animal enterprise to maintain a number of enterprises that will satisfy a variety of goals.

The complexity and inclusiveness of the farming systems concept forces research and extension staff to consider the same complexity of interdependent costs and benefits that confronts the farmer. If they understand why farmers make certain decisions, the staff may devise recommendations that can be accepted within the existing system. Much of the discrepancy between the technologies practiced by Malawi's smallholders and the technologies advocated by research and extension staff may be explained by the differences between the "real world" environment of the smallholder with its complex interdependencies and the controlled research plot environment where many variables are held constant and many others assumed to be irrelevant.

For example, research recommendations are made with the assumptions that farmers want to maximize yield per unit land and that farmers will devote as many resources as are needed for that specific enterprise. When those assumptions are true, the recommendations do help the farmer obtain very high yields. Often, however, smallholders are attempting to maximize several goals. They may want a secure food supply with several ingredients (*nsima* and *ndiwo* crops and animals or animal products for *ndiwo*) plus a cash income and therefore must compromise on their allocation of resources to each specific enterprise. In addition, because they grow many crops that demand attention during the single growing season, the smallholders must either hire additional labor or compromise on performing some cultivation tasks that demand simultaneous applications of labor.

Methodology

There are four general steps in any Farming Systems Research and Extension Program:

1. description and diagnosis,
2. designing alternative technologies,
3. testing the alternatives, and
4. extension (Gilbert, Norman, and Winch 1980).

Description and Diagnosis

The descriptive and diagnostic step includes several goals: to identify and understand the existing local farming systems; to identify recommendation domains, i.e., categories of farms and farmers that are homogeneous enough so that one set of recommendations will fit; and to identify circumstances within the systems where resources are not used as efficiently as possible. These would include compromises on technically optimum production technologies.

This first step involves reviewing secondary data (information collected by someone else) as well as conducting on-farm interviews and observations. Secondary information gives the research team background information about soil and rainfall patterns, population distribution, economic flows (crop and livestock sales, purchases of inputs, location of markets, availability of inputs), and existing research and extension recommendations and activities.

Extension staff are usually able to provide valuable information about local cropping patterns and, since they are in close contact with smallholders, information about smallholder complaints and the ways in which smallholder practices differ from recommendations. Interviews with extension staff must be supplemented by on-farm interviews and observations. Visits to smallholder farms and talks with small-holders permit the research team to appreciate the multiple objectives of smallholder farming and the resultant complexity. Interviewing farmers about their cropping patterns and decisions while actually standing in their fields allows the team to check verbal information with actual observation.

The interaction of research staff and smallholders is a consistent feature of farming systems research. Smallholder farmers are simultaneously the ultimate clients of this research and actual participants and partners in the research process. They are the ones who have a great deal of experience with local conditions and know what they are trying to accomplish with their multiple enterprises although they may not be able to articulate their goals. Therefore, the research team must actively encourage and support smallholder participation in describing, analyzing, prescribing, testing, and evaluating technologies and systems.

The incorporation of farmers and extension staff into research is part of the general methodology of farming systems research. Another part of the method is the use of multidisciplinary research teams. Since the unit that is being investigated (the farming system) is complex and includes a wide variety of factors, the research team includes production and socioeconomic staff from various disciplines.

The initial descriptive and diagnostic stage ends with the identification of high priority targets for adaptive research. Farming systems work is action-oriented. The team must constantly remind itself that the goal is rapid development of appropriate technology that smallholders can and will use. The single most important criterion for evaluating the success of the farming systems approach is the extent to which smallholders adopt technologies developed by the approach. Innovative technologies that are not adopted are failures. Nonadoption of the innovation probably means it is inappropriate for smallholders.

Designing Alternative Technologies

The second step is the design of alternative technologies. These alternatives are intended to improve the smallholder's exploitation of the biological potential of his or her environment and to enhance the farmer's overall utility/satisfaction (Collinson 1982). Based on the diagnosis of high priorities for research and on an understanding of the resource capabilities of farmers in the recommendation domain, the proposed alternatives are usually intended to modify the existing system rather than dramatically change it. The reason for this modest aim (gradual modification rather than radical change) is the recognition that smallholders are reluctant to undertake radical change that entails a lot of uncertainty. Although existing technologies may involve some biological inefficiencies, they are tested and well-understood by the local farmers.

Testing Alternative Technologies

The third step is testing the proposed alternatives to see how they perform. Although some testing might occur on research stations, an essential, preferred form of testing is on-farm and farmer-managed (Hildebrand and Poey 1985). When on-station trials are needed to evaluate some relationship under close controlled management, they are always supposed to be followed by on-farm trials to test the adaptability to farm conditions. Since FSR/E involves a complete adaptation to natural and socioeconomic conditions and the need to integrate any proposed technology into an ongoing complex system, farmers must necessarily manage the trials. Simply placing the trial on a farmer's land only tests adaptation to natural conditions. It is when smallholders actually manage the trials that they and the research team are best able to measure and evaluate the systems adaptability.

Farmer management entails some changes in trial design. For example, random bloc designs and designs with multiple repetitions are difficult for smallholder farmers to understand and operate. A more suitable design is when each treatment occurs only once per farm, and each farm is then considered a repetition of the trial.

Extension

The fourth step occurs when the tested innovation proves to be a good and acceptable modification of the system. At that time the proposal is handed over to the extension service. Note that extension is receiving a site-tested, adapted innovation that has been tested and approved by local farmers as well as through research. If the testing (third step) reveals problems, then the fourth step does not occur until the innovation is finally adaptable.

The fourth step is facilitated when extension staff are involved with the process of on-farm testing so that they are aware of the reasoning behind the process and the innovation. This accentuates once again the need to continually include extension staff and smallholders in a collaborative research program.

Extension is an essential step in the research process since adoption of the proposed alternative technologies is the single most important criterion by which the program will be evaluated. The best way to evaluate the success of the program is to resurvey the locality two or three years after starting the extension step to test how many smallholders are adopting the alternatives and to analyze any reasons for delays in adoption.

THE MALAWI AGRICULTURAL RESEARCH PROJECT

The above description of FSR/E concepts and methodology is abstract, just as a policy is abstract until it is implemented. In actual fact, FSR/E was introduced into Malawi as a component of a larger agricultural research project. During the processes of planning (1976–79) and implementing (1979–85), the theoretical design and concepts of FSR/E became subject to compromises and complications as the staff coped with institutional and personal issues and delays. The following brief description of the move from initial planning through beginning implementation illustrates some of the problems encountered.

The more we know about these problems, the more we can learn from our experiences. Programs as implemented are never as elegant and simple as the original policies and plans. In food policy terms, the decisionmaking environment of the implementing staff is always more complex than foreseen. In some ways its complexity parallels that of the farming systems decisionmaking environment that results in farmers making compromises in restructuring and allocating their productive resources.

The following brief timeline shows the lengthy process from a request for assistance to project implementation:

1976—Ministry of Agriculture (MOA) of Malawi began discussing with donor agencies an upgrading of the Department of Agricultural Research (DAR).
1978—United States Agency for International Development (USAID) completed a Project Identification Document (PID).
1978—University of Florida selected for project.
1979—University team, headed by a USAID officer, was sent to Malawi to design final project.
1980—USAID and UF sign final implementation agreement.

By the time Florida's Chief of Party arrived in Malawi, more than four years had elapsed between the government of Malawi's initial request for assistance and the beginning of the five-year (1980–85) Ministry of Agriculture/USAID/University of Florida Agricultural Research Project.

The FSR/E Component of the Project

Farming Systems Research and Extension was introduced into the project near the end of this process during the final design stage of the Project Paper in spring 1979. FSR/E was not originally included in the Project Identification Document, which described the project as one of general agricultural research. Since the composition of the design team was determined by this 1978 design document, no one was chosen to represent FSR/E on the design team. All of the university design team members were chosen for their disciplinary expertise (agronomy, agricultural economics, anthropology, etc.). Although I also had some experience and interest in the multidisciplinary farming systems approach, my original job description was to carry out the social soundness analysis and provide general support for other team members. However, with the concurrence of the other team members, I designed a FSR/E component that we added to the project.

The Malawi project was to be a general agricultural research project, based on disciplinary and commodity (specific crops and livestock) lines, with an added FSR/E component. Because the Project Identification Document had been the basis for Congress approving a general level of funding for the project, the USAID official heading the design team resisted our demands for additional funding. Consequently the FSR/E program was underfunded and understaffed from its inception. In the project design, only one person (a farming systems analyst) on the technical assistance team (TAT) implementing the project was to be directly responsible for the FSR/E program. While the other team members were directly responsible for their own disciplinary and/or commodity programs, they were to voluntarily collaborate with the farming systems analysis, i.e., be indirectly responsible. These conditions greatly reduced the multidisciplinary nature of the FSR/E program leadership.

The recruitment of TAT members for the Malawi Project created problems for the FSR/E program. Aside from the farming systems analyst (FSA), no others were recruited for their multidisciplinary interest or expertise. Only the FSA was recruited to work with the FSR/E program; the others were recruited to work in specific and separate disciplinary or commodity programs. In other words, the TAT members were neither recruited nor selected to function as a team. That failure was an important error, and the major problems faced by the FSR/E program in Malawi were related to the weakness of that team commitment.

Closely linked was the need for the FSR/E program to have strong joint leadership from both the technical and social sciences. Technical scientists sometimes view FSR/E as only a social science program and a way for social scientists to muscle into technical production territory where they are naive and a nuisance. Such opinions set the stage for conflict and opposition between the social and technical sciences rather than the cooperation FSR/E demands.

These problems were certainly present in Malawi, where only one member of the TAT, a social scientist, was directly in charge of FSR/E and essentially none of the other team members had received any positive FSR/E orientation prior to going to Malawi. Conflict and opposition were not continual, and the TAT team achieved many of its objectives, including the establishment of an FSR/E program (called Adaptive Research in Malawi). However, work would have proceeded more easily if multidisciplinary participation and leadership had been designed directly into the project. Voluntary collaboration is not enough.

Malawi is divided administratively into three regions: northern, central, and southern. The MOA is administratively decentralized into eight agricultural development divisions (ADDs), each of which has considerable autonomy. ADDs are subdivided into project areas, many of which have received separate funding from international agencies and have become integrated rural development projects (called RDPs in Malawi). RDPs are the basic agricultural development units because of their separate funding.

Based on the staffing and funding that were allocated to the FSR/E program, I anticipated the program working in three different sites the first year. For political reasons, the Ministry of Agriculture decided that one site should be located in each of the country's three regions. Background studies and diagnostic surveys were conducted in those three sites, but unexpected delays on hiring Malawian staff caused the program to be cut back, and on-site trials were planned and conducted in only two sites.

PHALOMBE 1981–1982

This section focuses on the work accomplished during 1981–1982 in Phalombe RDP, one of the three project sites in Malawi. (For additional information on population and cropping patterns, see Appendix I.)

Description and Diagnosis: The Diagnostic Survey

After several months of scheduling and reviewing ADD and RDP documents, a diagnostic survey was conducted in Phalombe in May 1981. FSR/E priorities differed in some ways from existing RDP and DAR policies.

The FSR/E program focused on the poor majority, whose highest priority was ensuring the staple food supply in addition to acquiring other foods and some cash income. Capital was scarce, and credit was feared because the poor had no security to cushion a bad cropping season and, therefore, feared the consequences of defaulting. Some households sold maize immediately after harvest because of a great need for money (for taxes, etc.), even though they knew food would run out later.

While some more fortunate smallholders had more land, capital, and security, FSR/E priorities emphasized the conditions faced by the majority. Policy suggestions by the FSR/E program were based on my belief that the best set of innovations permitted a step-by step progression with each step requiring a small change in resource commitment or risk.

The original extension and credit package in Phalombe was based on acre (0.4 hectare) production packages (integrated packages of seed and fertilizer that required a lot of capital and credit). In contrast, the FSR/E component suggested that the RDP promote credit for mini-packages of less than an acre size. The mini-packages would permit many more smallholders to participate in the project's credit program and receive seeds and fertilizers.

Similarly, the primary recommendations of the overall project emphasized the production of cash crops such as hybrid maize, tobacco, cotton, and rice and monocropping for all crops. The FSR/E program focused on improving the yield and stability of staple food production within a context of multiple cropping.

We also suggested that the project examine its extension coverage to see whether women smallholders were receiving enough extension advice. Women provided most of the labor on smallholder crops everywhere in Malawi (Clark 1975; Spring, Smith, and Kayuni 1983), but they were even more important in Phalombe where more than a third of all households were headed by women.

FSR/E further recommended that the project run a vaccination program to protect chickens, an important source of protein and cash income to many smallholders, from Newcastle disease.

Designing Alternative Technologies: Designing the Trials

The first staple testing was with the preferred and most common local staple, maize, to be followed by later trials with more drought-

Two Phalombe farmers receive seeds and fertilizer for on-farm trials. Clothing indicates income differences. Photograph by A. Hansen.

resistant sorghum and cassava. Basic research did not appear to be needed because the maize research program had already recommended a high-yielding variety (HYV) of maize and fertilizer package for semi-arid areas like Phalombe. Adaptive research trials were needed to test maize recommendations in intercropped situations on local farms under smallholder management to see how the recommendations fared under real conditions.

Testing Alternative Technologies: Implementing the Trials

DAR and Bunda College (University of Malawi) agronomists, ADD and RDP technical staff, the TAT farming systems analyst, and Phalombe farmers all actively participated in planning the on-farm, farmer-managed trials in Phalombe. First the professionals worked out the design. Public meetings were called in the two villages where the trials would be conducted, and farmers were consulted. In fact, the trial design was modified to incorporate smallholder suggestions.

Since smallholders needed to be able to understand and manage the trial, standard complex agronomic designs were not used. Final plans called for a simple two-by-two factorial test of two maize varieties with and without fertilizer, all four treatments with the same intercropping mixture of maize, cowpeas, and sunflowers. Each farmer had only the four treatments, no replications, and the farmers were treated as blocks for statistical analysis. The two maizes tested were the "local" and the composite HYV variety developed and recommended by DAR. To use no fertilizer was the common practice; the other fertilizer level was the recommended one for the HYV composite: 30 kilos of nitrogen per hectare applied as 20:20:0 (base dressing) and sulfate of ammonia (side dressing).

The trial farmers were split almost equally between smaller and larger, women and men, and married and unmarried women. The total sample consisted of sixteen farmers, eight from each of two villages. One part of each farmer's field was subdivided into four plots, each four ridges wide (3.2 meters) and ten maize stations long (9 meters). Two plots were to be planted with each type of maize, fertilizers being applied to one plot of each maize. Verbal explanations were supplemented with tracing diagrams in the dirt, and many questions had to be answered before people were satisfied that they understood what was

Phalombe farmers receiving instruction concerning on-farm trials and means for evaluating costs and benefits. Photograph by A. Hansen.

going to happen and why. As an additional guide, signs were given to each farmer to mark each plot, and they were abbreviated in the Chichewa language instead of the usual scientific coding. *MAK* stood for *chimanga cha makolo* or local maize, *CCA* for the composite, and *-F* for the plots with *feteliza* or fertilizer.

Seeds, fertilizer, a regulation cup for applying the fertilizer, and signs to mark the plots were distributed at a later meeting. The research design was explained again as was financial information about the inputs: prices at the government market and the size of the bags in which they were sold. Correct timing for applying fertilizers to maize was discussed and, when someone commented on the unusual color of the CCA seeds, I explained that they had been coated with a poisonous chemical. This discussion turned out to be important because, when planting was delayed in one village, an elderly woman ate the local maize seed because she was hungry. She then told us that she would have eaten the CCA seeds also if she had not heard from us about the poisonous coating.

The farmers provided the actual labor and management for the trial. Each of them was visited weekly by a local research or extension agent, and each month the FSR/E team visited from the headquarters research station near Lilongwe, the capital city. Weekly visits noted the dates of significant operations (plantings, weedings, fertilizer applications) and natural occurrences (rain, attack of army worms, etc.) and the condition of the treatments. The agents also offered advice concerning the trial plots.

During the monthly visits, we inspected the trial plots, interviewed the trial farmers about their reactions, and continued investigations into Phalombe farming systems. During each visit, the farming systems staff met with RDP management and staff to talk about the progress of the trials; this continual interaction between research and extension was necessary to ensure that extension staff understood the trials and could confidently extend the outcome to smallholders.

In February, a special multiple cropping survey was conducted to supplement data collected in the original farming systems survey. Although the 1981–82 trial used a standard intercropping pattern in all four treatments, intercropping was a variable that needed to be investigated in future trials.

The farmers in one village suffered through an early drought that forced eight farmers to replant their maize in late December, a month later than the usual planting time and a damaging blow in an area where the rain often stops too early. When the rain came, so did erosion, and two of the trial plots were washed away because people were cultivating hillside slopes. Army worms attacked many areas of Phalombe that year, including that village, and there were the usual stalkborers and termites to combat in both villages. We had originally intended not to use any pesticides to give all of the farmers the opportunity to see how the treatments responded in various ecological niches, but we changed our minds when the army worms attacked.

Since smallholders were more accustomed to evaluating or measuring volumes than weights, yields were measured both ways, using a scale for weight and a standard calibrated tin for volume. After all of the plots were harvested, another meeting was called in each village to discuss everyone's evaluations of the different treatments (*see* Hansen, Mwango, and Phiri 1982 for smallholder perceptions).

Table 1

Maize Yields from Phalombe On-Farm, Farm-Managed Trial, 1981–1982
(Usable Grain Yield in Metric Tons per Hectare)

	1	2	3	4	5	6	7	8	Mean
				First Village					
Four Treatments				8 Farmers					
Local maize (LM)	2.2	2.2	1.9	1.2	1.3	0.9	1.0	0.5	1.4
Fertilized local maize (LM-F)	3.6	3.7	4.3	3.2	2.3	2.3	3.1	2.8	3.2
Composite maize (CCA)	3.5	2.0	2.9	0.4	0.6	0.5	0.6	0.3	1.3
Fertilized composite maize (CCA-F)	5.0	4.7	4.3	3.5	2.4	1.7	3.0	2.8	3.4
Mean for farmer	3.6	3.2	3.3	2.1	1.7	1.3	1.9	1.6	2.3
				Second Village					
Four Treatments				6 Farmers					
Local maize (LM)	1.8	1.1	1.6	1.0	1.6	0.6			1.3
Fertilized local maize (LM-F)	3.2	2.5	2.9	1.2	1.9	0.8			2.1
Composite maize (CCA)	2.2	0.7	0.9	0.3	1.1	0.3			0.9
Fertilized composite maize (CCA-F)	2.9	2.5	2.1	1.1	0.8	0.4			1.6
Mean for farmer	2.5	1.7	1.9	0.9	1.4	0.5			1.5

Trial Results

The yields from the plots of eight farmers in one village and six in another are included in the analysis (two plots being omitted due to erosion and poor germination; *see* Table 1). The statistics represent metric tons per hectare (MT/ha) of usable grain. Usable grain was defined by the smallholders themselves as they worked with us to shell and weigh the harvest. They eliminated all rotten grain and that which was very badly eaten away by weevils. As noted by DAR, smallholder criteria for defining usable and unusable grain differed from the criteria used by laboratory technicians, who discarded all grain that had been attacked at all by insects (DAR Crop Storage Research Section).

Obvious differences were observed (1) between the means for villages, (2) between the means for farmers in each village, and (3) between the means for the two fertilizer levels in the first village. The highly significant difference between the two villages is easily explained. Both villages planted in late November, but the second village did not receive enough rain at that time to sustain the seedlings and had to replant in late December, after their first real planting rains. The first village received enough rain in late November and early December, so their maize had a month's headstart. The second village also suffered severe attacks by army worms in January, but the worms were less a factor than the rain and time of planting. Yields in the first village, therefore, showed how the treatments responded to better conditions. Yields in the second village reflected the adverse conditions that continually threatened Phalombe agriculture.

Both maizes responded strongly to fertilizer. Both local and CCA more than doubled their yields in the first village (with its better conditions), although the effect of fertilizer was not as marked in the second village (with its generally poorer performance). To our surprise there was little difference between the two maizes at either level of fertilizer in the first village under better conditions, and local maize performed somewhat better in the second village under poorer conditions.

It was important that the technical scientists accepted the trial results, and the TAT maize breeder was asked for advice about how to proceed with further statistical analysis. He suggested the analysis of variance (ANOVA). This analysis apportioned total variance among the treatments, the blocs (farmers), and the individual values (random error); the higher the mean square the greater the variance attributed to that factor (Table 2). In analysis of the combined villages, the villages were used as blocks and the farmers as replications of each block. The F ratio expressed the difference between the mean squares of that factor and of error; the higher the ratio, the more unlike were the populations. The significance statistic (Table 2) expressed the probability that such a difference was not caused by chance.

The effect of fertilizer was highly significant in the first and in the combined villages and significant in the second village. Maize types were never significant. The differences among farmers were significant

Table 2
Analyses of Variance Results

Source of Variance	Degrees of Freedom	Mean Square	F Ratio	Significance
		First Village		
Farmers (8)	7	3.947	2.41	94%
Fertilizer (2)	1	25.740	15.74	>99%
Maize type (2)	1	0.428	0.26	—*
Fertilizer × Maize	1	—*		
Error	21	1.635		
		Second Village		
Farmers (6)	5	2.049	3.53	97%
Fertilizer (2)	1	3.450	5.94	97%
Maize type (2)	1	1.000	1.72	—*
Fertilizer × Maize	1	0.010	—*	
Error	15	0.581		
		Combined Villages		
Villages (2)	1	11.550	10.83	>99%
Fertilizer (2)	1	25.515	23.93	>99%
Maize type (2)	1	0.026	—*	
Villages × Fertilizer	1	3.676	3.45	93%
Villages × Maize	1	1.403	1.32	—*
Fertilizer × Maize	1	—*		
Error	49	1.066		

Note: In the analyses for the individual villages, the smallholders are used as blocks, and there is only one replication of each treatment per block. In the analysis of the combined villages, the villages are used as blocks, and there are eight replications (farmers) in the first village/block and six in the second.

An asterisk (*) indicates insignificant result.

in each village, and the difference between the two villages (explained above by reference to rainfall and time of planting) was highly significant. Differences among farmers will be addressed after first discussing the maize-type-versus-fertilizer issue.

The importance of fertilizer to maize yields was obvious, but the insignificant relationship between maize type and yield needed to be examined more closely. Maize type and fertilizer relationships were also studied in yield data collected by the ADD Evaluation Unit for the 1980–81 National Sample Survey of Agriculture (Table 3). More than

Table 3
Smallholder Maize Yield by Fertilizer: Phalombe, 1980–1981

Fertilizer Application (kilograms per hectare)	Number of Plots	Local Maize Yield (metric tons per hectare)	Composite (UCA) Maize Yields (metric tons per hectare)
None	431	0.8	1.8 for 12 plots throughout the
1–49	5	1.6	Phalombe Project
50–99	21	1.3	
100–149	22	1.3	
150–199	19	1.4	1.5 when plots in one area with
200–249	6	1.9	highest rainfall are excluded
250–299	4	2.0	
300–349	6	1.9	
350+	6	1.2	

Source: Evaluation Unit, Blantyre ADD.

five hundred smallholder maize plots in Phalombe were sampled during that cropping season (Table 3), although very few (only twelve) plots in their sample grew anything other than local maize. All of those twelve were UCA, another composite similar to CCA. That data showed a significant difference in mean yield between local and UCA, but that difference appeared to be largely a matter of differential fertilizer application rates. Comparisons were also made between maize types at similar levels of fertilizer (Table 3). Recommended levels of fertilizer for composites were 3 bags per acre or 7.5 bags (375 kilograms) per hectare. Local maize yields equaled the mean for UCA once 200 kilograms per hectare were applied.

Yield Stability

Another important dimension was yield stability. Farmers wanted higher yields and a more secure or stable production. More stability may be defined as reduced variability; relative stability of the two maize types was examined by looking at the range of yields (Table 1). The coefficients of variation (c.v.) measured the extent to which the individual yield values deviated from the mean (Table 4). This statistic was corrected for the magnitude of the different means (c.v. = standard

Table 4
Yield Stability as Measured by Coefficients of Variation (c.v.)

First Village		Second Village		Both Villages	
Treatment	c.v.	Treatment	c.v.	Treatment	c.v.
Local Maize	45	Local Maize	35	Local Maize	39
Fertilized Local	22	Fertilized Local	45	Fertilized Local	35
Composite Maize	98	Composite Maize	78	Composite Maize	88
Fertilized Composite	34	Fertilized Composite	63	Fertilized Composite	52

deviation divided by the mean), so all of the values in Table 4 were directly comparable; the higher the c.v., the more variable and unstable. Except for the local variety in the second village, both maizes were more stable when fertilized, a feature most noticeable in the first village under better growing conditions. Local maize was more stable than CCA in each village and under both fertilizer conditions. The inverse of stability may be defined as responsiveness, and CCA seemed to be more responsive to its environment, whether adverse or favorable.

Both yield and stability improved with fertilizer. Unfortunately, fertilizer was a costly input, and lack of capital and fear of credit inhibited people from high cost inputs. The government marketing agency (ADMARC) sold inputs to smallholders and purchased their maize. Recommended levels of fertilizer cost 61.25 Malawian Kwacha (MK 61.25) based on an ADMARC price of MK 8.50 per 50 kilogram bag of 20:20:0 (2.5 bags) and MK 8 per bag of S/A (55 bags). Recommended seeding rates for CCA cost MK 6.25 per hectare, based on a price of MK 2.50 per 10 kilogram bag (2.25 bags needed). In 1982 ADMARC bought maize for MK 0.11 (11 tambala) per kilogram or MK 110 per metric ton (MT). Thus a yield increase of 0.6 MT/ha was more than enough to offset the cost of fertilizer, and 0.1 MT/ha would pay the CCA seed costs. The analysis shows that it was profitable to apply fertilizer to both types of maize in both villages, although there was little average profit in the second village (Table 5).

Farmer Heterogeneity

Thus far, the analysis had only examined aggregates and means. Differences among farmers were very important and, in this instance,

Table 5
Profitability of Fertilizer Application to Maize
(Metric Tons per Hectare)

	First Village		Second Village	
Maize Type	Yield Increase with Fertilizer	Profit	Yield Increase with Fertilizer	Profit
Local	1.8	+1.2	0.8	+0.2
Composite	2.1	+1.5	0.7	+0.1

Note: Each metric ton is worth 110 Malawi Kwacha at 1982 prices.

statistically significant (Table 2). This fact is illustrated by Table 6 that plots the mean yields of unfertilized and then fertilized maize, combining local and CCA varieties, for all fourteen farmers. There was no normal distribution tailing off to either or both extremes. Instead, there were essentially two categories of farmers in each of the two villages, low-yielding and high-yielding. This division held true with or without fertilizer.

Three farmers in the first village (1, 2, 3) and one in the second (A) (Table 6) distinguished themselves by high yields without fertilizer, producing more than double the yield of the majority of the farmers in the sample. Fertilizer improved all of the yields in the first village, but the same three farmers remained far in front. The high-yielding farmer (A) in the second village maintained an early lead in his own village (Table 6) but fell behind the high-yielding farmers in the first village (1, 2, 3), presumably because of the poor rainfall, pests, etc., which plagued the second village.

More ominous was the failure of half of the farmers in the second village (D, E, F) (Table 6) to reap any significant advantage from fertilizer. All three would have lost money by buying and applying fertilizer. The relationship between crop failures or very poor yields and unprofitable returns from applying fertilizer was clear. The fact that even fertilizer was not a safe recommendation for everyone probably explains why FSR/E surveys throughout Malawi had found that smallholders consistently delayed applying fertilizer past the recommended time. They were probably waiting until they were able to judge the rains and health of the crop before committing such an expensive input.

Table 6
Smallholder Yields by Village Fertilizer Treatment

	First Village		Second Village	
Range of Yields	No Fertilizer	With Fertilizer	No Fertilizer	With Fertilizer
4.0 < 4.5		1, 2, 3		
3.5 < 4.0				
3.0 < 3.5		4, 7		A
2.5 < 3.0	1	8		B, C
2.0 < 2.5	2, 3	5, 6	A	
1.5 < 2.0				
1.0 < 1.5			C, E	D, E
0.5 < 1.0	4, 5, 6, 7		B, D	F
0.0 < 0.58	8		F	

Note: Maize yields (metric tons per hectare) represent averages of both maize varieties. Farmers in the second village are coded by letters in this table rather than by numbers for ease of presentation.

Two Recommendation Domains

Looking at the differences among farmers led to seeing the differential utility of the composite HYV and the existence of two recommendation domains. Although aggregate data showed no yield difference between maize types, adopting the HYV made real sense for the three most successful farmers in the first village (1, 2, 3). These three got high yields from both varieties, with and without fertilizer, but they consistently got better yields from the composite and demonstrated the advantage of CCA over local in high-yielding situations. There was an obvious relationship between the "good" farmers and the suitability of the HYV.

While the three good farmers had success with the HYV, the other five farmers in the same village harvested 0.6 MT/ha or less on their plots of unfertilized CCA, severely depressing the mean for that treatment. Their plots showed no differences between maizes or, with the lowest yields, the advantage of local stability. When the added cost to buy the CCA seed was considered, equal to the income from 0.1 MT/ha, it was obvious that the HYV was not recommended for these farmers. Shifting to the HYV would not be profitable for them given their yields. The same conclusion was applicable to everyone in the second village with the possible exception of the first farmer.

The analysis suggested that the majority of farmers in this section of Phalombe would not profit in yield or in stability of yield by adopting the recommended HYV, but the minority of good farmers would profit. The minority who got high yields from all treatments constituted one recommendation domain, and extension could continue with confidence to advise them to adopt the HYV and fertilizer package. On the other hand, the majority of farmers was a separate recommendation domain. For whatever reason, the "recommended" HYV was not recommendable to this domain at this time. This conclusion and these data have been elaborated elsewhere (Hansen, Mwango, and Phiri 1982; Hansen 1986; Hildebrand 1984; Hildebrand and Poey 1985).

Some factor or factors interfered with yields in general on the fields of the majority of farmers. The yield data (Table 4) could not satisfactorily explain the gap in yields between the two farmer categories or the low yields of the majority because the trial had been designed to measure differences among treatments rather than among farmers. Each farmer was statistically a separate block, and each block had its unique location, microclimate, soils, field history, and farmer. For convenience, the interference factors were lumped into a "farmer husbandry" category.

Interview data gave some clues. Differential residual fertilizer was a factor since two of the best farmers (1, 2) had planted fertilized tobacco in the on-farm trial fields the previous year. Husbandry was also a factor; some farmers spent more time and care on their fields while others spent less time, were sick or old and weak, had domestic problems which diminished labor availability, etc. The highest-yielding farmers (1, 2, 3, A) were male, usually high status, usually tobacco growers, and had larger amounts of land than the others. These differences among smallholders needed to be investigated in further trials.

On-farm testing had shown its scientific usefulness in this instance, but a key had been the selection criteria for the sample farmers. Most of the Phalombe trial farmers conformed in scale and sex to the majority for whom recommendations were being sought. Previous on-farm trials in Malawi had consistently shown the advantage of the HYVs over local maizes, but the farmers in those trials had always been good farmers.

This FSR/E trial included a broad range of smallholders and showed that the best farmers in Phalombe were a separate recommendation domain. The previous smallholder samples in other on-farm trials had not been representative of the majority, but DAR had assumed that results from those trials were applicable to all smallholders. One implication of the Phalombe results was that agricultural researchers had to question that assumption. Specifically, HYVs had been assumed on the basis of previous trials to be recommendable to all farmers, but that assumption now had to be questioned.

Previous variety and husbandry recommendations in Malawi had been very general, many aimed at the national level and other broad subdivisions determined by ecological factors such as rainfall, altitude, and temperature. Research and extension staff had known that the recommendations had to be drawn more exactly, and the DAR was in the long process of doing that in coordination with the ADDs and RDPs. Only biological and climatic factors were being considered, however, not socioeconomic differences among farmers. The Phalombe trial demonstrated the importance of intralocality variation among smallholders and the usefulness of the FSR/E approach. Socioeconomic variation needed to be considered in revising agricultural recommendations.

Evaluating the Trials

Although the trial had not been designed to identify or discriminate among farmer husbandry factors, the trial had succeeded in testing under realistic smallholder conditions a set of "traditional" inputs. Local maize grown without fertilizer was a popular tradition while CCA and fertilizers were scientific traditions (Shils 1981). Reality testing had confirmed one scientific tradition, the use of fertilizers, and provided surprising insights into the differential utility of the two maize traditions.

CONCLUSIONS: LEARNING FROM EXPERIENCE

Those of us involved in the Phalombe trials learned several lessons: smallholder farmers may be heterogeneous in critical aspects that are not immediately obvious to outsiders. Recommended innovations in production technology, including the choice of high-yielding varieties, may not be appropriate for all farmers because of the heterogeneity. Sometimes the recommended innovations are even counterproductive for certain farmers. More research is needed to discover what works for whom.

FSR/E provides insights into these differences among farmers. Technical research that only examines physical and nonhuman factors will miss the important socioeconomic factors that are essential determinants of a farmer's decisionmaking environment. Methodological considerations in selecting trial farmers and sites may reveal or conceal important variations among farmers. Technical research scientists are not skilled in these methods or trained to recognize and analyze these socioeconomic factors, so socioeconomic scientists need to be involved in agricultural research. On-farm trials and farmer participation in trial design and implementation complement research-controlled trials and help ensure that research recommendations will make sense in farmers' systems.

Food policy wants to influence the decisionmaking environments of food producers (and others). Effective food policies and influences must be based on an accurate understanding of the existing environments. Thus, effective food policies must include FSR/E and on-farm trials within their national research programs.

The farming systems approach considers a wider range of factors and relationships than more traditional research and extension approaches —which commonly focus on single crops, animals, or other elements (pests, soils, machinery, etc.). However, a farming systems program does not replace the single-factor programs; both approaches are needed to complement each other. The more narrowly focused programs pursue in depth specific, technical relationships (Figure 1), while the broader, more comprehensive farming systems program examines the extent to which existing recommendations are appropriate for smallholders, identifies high priority research projects for other research programs, and helps establish procedures to test the adaptability of possible innovations to smallholder conditions and goals.

Commodity specific or discipline-specific approaches are more idealistic. They construct ideal or optimum biological solutions to the problem of increasing one characteristic, yield. The farming systems

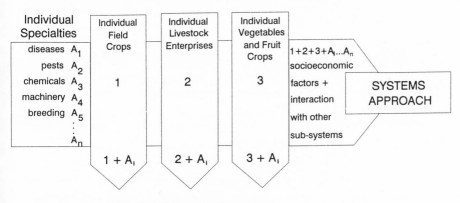

Figure 1
Traditional and Farming Systems Approaches

approach is more practical. It emphasizes adaptive research to discover which alternative solutions are most suitable to actual small farmer conditions, resources, and constraints. This is adaptive research in a complex sense because it includes adaptation to natural and socioeconomic circumstances as well as the interaction of enterprises on a farm. A farming systems research program is, therefore, a vital component of the total research effort that specifically addresses smallholder needs and constraints.

At another level, that of the project rather than the farmer's field, there are other lessons. The politics of research needs to be made more explicit. The ways projects are structured and technical assistance personnel recruited (as well as personal characteristics of the individuals involved) affect whether the research scientists and extension staff work together or oppose each other. FSR/E requires cooperative teamwork from a multidisciplinary team, and this sort of teamwork is rare anywhere (Hansen and McMillan 1986:3–6). Moreover, while commodity researchers and FSR/E may be focused on actions within a farmer's field, the researchers and their programs work within an administrative environment that is competitive and political. Politics and strife accompany FSR/E because it cuts across disciplinary and departmental boundaries, thereby trespassing on many territories.

Livestock Development, Policy Issues, and Anthropology in East Africa

J. Terrance McCabe

The development of the livestock industry in the arid rangelands of East Africa has proved to be an exceptionally difficult task for the international development community. Donor agencies and research organizations are beginning to retreat from the position that livestock productivity can be significantly increased in regions where pastoral nomadism has been the traditional form of livestock husbandry. Because many "experts" have seen the major obstacles to the implementation of successful livestock development projects in Africa primarily in social rather than technological terms (pastoralists have not cooperated or done what was expected), the anthropologists who participated in these projects run the risk of being classified as ineffectual to development planners. This trend is a reversal of that seen in other development contexts where the role of anthropologists is increasingly valued.

In this chapter I examine the reasons behind this development failure and argue that project design based on poorly defined policy objectives and misconceived assumptions about pastoral ecosystems have limited anthropological input to little more than documenting the repeated failures.

The literature relating to East African pastoralism and development is voluminous; books by Raikes (1981), Galaty et al. (1981), Jahnke (1982), Sandford (1983), and Simpson and Evangelou (1984), as well as numerous book chapters and articles, have all considered some aspects of the overall problem. The authors differ significantly about root causes and potential solutions to the problem of East African livestock development. I hope to bring together the literature in such a way that a few unambiguous points can serve as a reference point for future development efforts.

I have spent most of the past twelve years researching, conducting fieldwork, and writing about pastoral people in East Africa, especially the Turkana of northwestern Kenya. My development experience has involved assessing the impact of development-related activities on traditional systems of livestock management, especially in relation to drought response. Many friends and colleagues have been involved in research related to livestock development, especially in conjunction with the International Livestock Center for Africa (ILCA). Thus, I am approaching this problem from the perspective of an interested observer rather than that of an insider.

The following chapter has five objectives:

1. to present some of the critical features of East African ecology and pastoral production systems,
2. to trace some of the more significant changes and policy decisions which relate to livestock development,
3. to discuss some of the relevant features of anthropological writing and fieldwork as it pertains to East African pastoral people,
4. to demonstrate how policy decisions and assumptions about arid land ecosystems have resulted in project designs which have little chance of success, and
5. to discuss some recent literature which suggests that an alternative paradigm for livestock development may be possible.

EAST AFRICAN ECOLOGY AND PASTORAL PRODUCTION SYSTEMS

The following discussion focuses on the arid and semiarid regions of East Africa—where the raising of livestock incorporates mobility and extensive land use. Although I occasionally draw on examples of pastoral development from Uganda, I focus more on Tanzania and especially on Kenya. The reason for doing so lies both on geography and ecology (Uganda is wetter with more land classified as suitable for agricultural than for rangeland development) and on practicality (there is more information available relating to livestock development in Kenya than elsewhere).

Throughout the arid and semiarid regions of Africa, human popula-

Table 1
Land Classification in Kenya and Tanzania

		Kenya		Tanzania	
Ecological Zone		Square Kilometers (thousands)	Percentage	Square Kilometers (thousands)	Percentage
1, 2	High Agricultural Potential	54	9	40	5
3	Medium Agricultural Potential	58	10	255	29
4	Marginal Agricultural Potential	56	10	303	34
5	Medium Range	300	51	282	32
6	Semi Desert	112	20	—	—
Total		580	100	880	100

Source: Raikes 1981

tions have traditionally relied on livestock to supply a significant portion of their subsistence needs. In the more arid regions, people's economies often are based exclusively on the raising of livestock, as, for example, in the Ngisonyoka Turkana of Kenya. As the amount of moisture available to plants increases, human populations increasingly base their economies on crop production, which is more ecologically efficient, and may or may not incorporate livestock husbandry into the household economy. Although there is some lack of agreement about the amount of annual precipitation necessary for sustained agriculture, it is safe to say that livestock-based economies dominate in areas which receive less than 750 mm of rainfall per year (Pratt 1984). These areas are commonly classified as rangelands or deserts, and Eastern Africa is composed primarily of land which falls within these classifications. More than 80 percent of Kenya and 65 percent of Tanzania is composed of land suited for little other than raising livestock (Table 1).

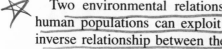 Two environmental relationships influence the manner in which human populations can exploit arid and semiarid rangelands: (1) an inverse relationship between the amount of precipitation and the reliability of precipitation, and (2) a direct relationship between the amount of precipitation and the amount of primary production produced by

the natural vegetation of the range. The presence of these relationships means that forage resources in such areas are unpredictable both spatially and temporally. In addition there are many constraints to efficient exploitation of vegetal resources because of lack of water, presence of disease, or lack of security. *traditionally*

Traditionally, East African pastoral people have adapted to these environmental conditions by raising multiple species herds, moving frequently, and incorporating a high degree of flexibility in the organization of human groups. The articulation among the pattern of mobility, the aggregation and dispersion of human and livestock populations, the spatial distribution of natural resources (especially forage and water), and the temporal parameters of these resources contribute to diversity among East African pastoral peoples. A series of common attributes can be found among most if not all pastoral people inhabiting the East African rangelands.

Traditional livestock production systems are primarily subsistence dairy operations (Brown 1971; Dyson-Hudson 1986). Although all East African pastoral people incorporate grain products into their household economy (either through purchase, barter, or cultivation), data on pastoral diets and age/sex structures of herds all confirm that the principal subsistence use of livestock is to supply milk (Dyson-Hudson 1986). All East African livestock production systems require high inputs of labor which vary seasonally and require a high degree of local knowledge and management skill. Livestock are typically managed by members of an extended family under the direction of the senior male. One of the principal tasks of the herd owner is to match the needs of the livestock, in terms of forage, water, and security, with the nutritional needs of the people. Thus animals and people are often shifted among mobile camps as circumstances warrant. Livestock may be separated along species-specific or production-specific lines and managed independently, often with only occasional contact with the herd owner.

For example, among the Turkana, extended family members along with all the livestock constitute a single household (the *awi*) during the rainy season. As the dry season begins, the herd owner may choose to separate his cattle from the rest of the livestock because they need to graze on grasses which are more abundant in the mountains than on the plains. Typically the cattle will be managed by an adult son or brother of the herd owner. As the dry season progresses, the herd owner may

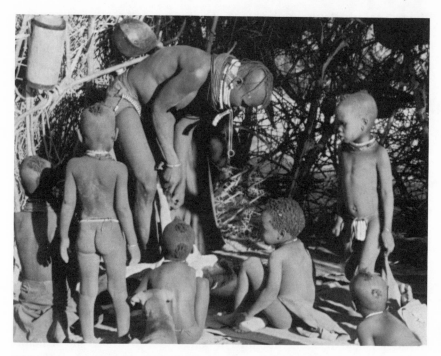

Turkana woman and her family. Photograph by J. T. McCabe.

then separate his milking camels and small stock from the nonmilking camels and small stock. The nonmilking camels and the nonmilking small stock will then be separated from the *awi* and managed separately, again under the care of an adult son or other close adult male relative. Each separate herd then follows a unique migration pattern and may be out of contact with the herd owner for months at a time.

Production units seasonally aggregate into temporary associations, commonly referred to in the literature as neighborhoods, which congregate when forage resources are abundant and disperse as the resource base diminishes (Evans-Pritchard 1940; Gulliver 1955; Dyson-Hudson 1966). Production units are usually grouped into loose associations referred to as sections or subsections, which often define the boundaries within which all members have open access to forage resources. Sections may be part of a larger political organization usually referred to as a tribe but which rarely acts in a corporate fashion (Evans-Pritchard 1940; Gulliver 1955).

Political organization is, in general, decentralized and allows a high degree of autonomy to individual herd owners. While the elderly and the wealthy accrue respect and political power which allows them to influence the behavior of others, they cannot dictate another's particular course of action.

A critical feature of all East African pastoral societies (as well as most if not all African pastoral societies) is the network of relatives and friends to which an individual is bound through a series of reciprocal rights and obligations involving the exchange of livestock and labor. It is to this network that an individual herd owner turns when he needs help, especially following livestock losses—commonly resulting from drought, raiding, or disease.

Typically, forage resources are free to all members of the section, but access to water is not. For example, among the Ngisonyoka all individuals have access to water in the rivers when flowing and in open pools found in the riverbeds as the water is receding. However, in areas where wells are dug through sand, clay, and occasionally rock, access to water is restricted to members of the family of the individuals who dug the well. Free access to forage and restricted access to water appear to be common features of most, if not all, pastoral societies in East Africa (for more information see Dyson-Hudson and McCabe 1985; Edwards, Classen, and Schroten 1983).

LIVESTOCK DEVELOPMENT IN EASTERN AFRICA

The need to increase livestock productivity is based on some rather harsh but widely accepted projections. Sub-Saharan Africa's human population is expected to double by the year 2000, to grow from 347 million to 639 million (Simpson and McDowell 1986, Simpson 1984). It has been estimated that if the human population were to consume livestock products at the current rate, the livestock population would have to increase from 147 million cattle to 280 million cattle, and sheep and goats from 230 million animals to 410 million animals (Simpson 1984). Policy decisions directed at the goal of increased livestock production are understandable on a continent in which many people are already in need of additional protein and countries are in need of export goods.

Unfortunately, the one fact that stands out in any discussion of livestock development in Sub-Saharan Africa is the nearly consistent record of failure despite the investment of millions of dollars. McDowell says of the period 1968–83: "To meet a rapid rise in demand for additional livestock products, African governments have invested an average of about $1 billion per year over the past 15 years in the attempt to improve pastoral production systems. But despite this apparent large input, assistance agencies and governments concur, in general, that results have been disappointing" (McDowell 1984:44).[1] Goldschmidt summarizes a review of pastoral development projects, stating that "The picture that emerges is one of almost unrelieved failure. Nothing seems to work, few pastoral lives have improved, there is no evidence of increased production of meat and milk, the land continues to deteriorate, and millions of dollars have been spent" (Goldschmidt 1981:116). Similar statements by Dyson-Hudson (1986), Jahnke (1982), Sandford (1983), Horowitz (1986), and Horowitz and Little (1987) illustrate a rare case of agreement among academics, as well as agreement between academics and planners. An outline of some of the more salient features of the historical sequence of livestock development projects in East Africa helps illustrate the reasons behind these failures and why anthropological input has had little effect.

The Colonial Period

The development of the livestock industry in East Africa had its roots in the livestock epizootics of the 1890s.[2] During this period rinderpest killed most of the region's cattle. This disease outbreak was followed by smallpox, famine, and war throughout the pastoral areas in East Africa. One of the most important impacts of these serial disasters was the abandonment of much of the rangelands by the indigenous people at the same time that European colonists were migrating into eastern Africa. This development was especially important in Kenya where most of the high potential rangeland was open to European settlement in the early twentieth century. The occupation and subsequent development of these areas by Europeans, the restrictions they imposed on the pastoralists' movement, and their failure to develop the poor rangelands formed the foundation for Kenya's livestock development policy until after World War II.

In contrast, in Tanzania—which had neither as extensive a settler community as Kenya nor the high grade cattle to protect—the development policy promoted during the period prior to World War II was designed to improve livestock productivity throughout the country. Government policy focused on the eradication of disease, primarily rinderpest and contagious bovine pleuropneumonia.

Following World War II, the colonial governments reversed their earlier policies towards African livestock production by introducing veterinary care and encouraging increased marketing; this effort was far more pronounced in Tanzania (then Tanganyika) than in Kenya. The introduction of veterinary care was considered necessary because quarantine restrictions were not able to prevent the spread of livestock disease into the European-held herds. Moreover, since government officials had been complaining about overgrazing in the pastoral areas for years (Spencer 1965), a program of compulsory destocking was introduced which would both protect the land and supply cattle to a new meat-canning factory at Athi river (forced destocking was not new to some pastoral areas, for the British used this means to punish unruly pastoralists in the early days of their administration).

The decade following the end of the war witnessed a continuation of government policies which incorporated compulsory destocking, improvements in access to veterinary services, and in some instances, the drilling of boreholes and the building of small catchment dams. During the mid-1950s a new policy which incorporated restrictions on the number of animals allowed on the range coupled with range improvements began to be instituted in both Kenya and Tanzania. By the early 1960s many of these "grazier" schemes began to fail, reportedly because of the "lack of discipline" on the part of the pastoralists (Raikes 1981).

Since Independence

Livestock development schemes implemented after independence followed a similar model of incorporating restrictions on movement and limitations on the number of animals which the range could support. During the late 1960s, 1970s, and 1980s governments and donor agencies implemented a variety of projects in an attempt to make the rangelands more productive. The basis of livestock development for the period 1969–81 in Kenya was outlined in the Kenya Livestock Development Project (KLDP): "The Kenya Livestock Development Project was initiated in 1969 to enhance the development of livestock production in Kenya. The objectives are to increase meat production, enhance employment in the livestock sector, encourage a more equitable income distribution, contribute to the country's foreign exchange earnings, ensure the conservation of the country's range resources and improve technical services to the livestock industry" (ILCA 1979:3).

It is impossible to describe in this space all of the range improvements coupled with marketing policy decisions and restrictions on human and livestock populations in Kenya since independence. However, Dyson-Hudson's account of the Kenya Livestock Development Project, which lasted for five years in the 1960s and early 1970s, illustrates the scale of investment. Dyson-Hudson counted 203 individual and group ranches, 29 cooperative ranches, and 96 community grazing schemes, involving a total of 14.3 million acres and an investment of approximately 26 million dollars (Dyson-Hudson 1986). Although unique to Kenya, the Kenya Livestock Development Project was typical of the development strategies of the period (*see* Doornbos and Lofchie 1971 for an account of the Ankole Ranching Scheme in Uganda). These strategies typically emphasized one or a combination of the following: improved marketing, better transport, disease prevention, water installation, breeding improvements, rangeland quality, or rotational grazing. The attempt to limit livestock numbers to the "carrying capacity" of the range and a general failure to achieve the objects for which such projects were intended united these post-independence projects.[3]

WHY HAVE THESE SCHEMES FAILED?

Although I have previously quoted a number of authors regarding the failure of livestock development projects, failure can be defined in many terms. Perhaps a simple analysis of the "leading indicators" of livestock production in Africa most effectively illustrates how little has actually been achieved since independence (Table 2).

For example, while the leading indicators show that livestock production did not keep pace with the expanding human population, from the perspective of national governments "failed" projects throughout Africa may have had successful side benefits such as improved access to health services or the settlement of nomadic communities. However,

Table 2
Leading Indicators for Livestock Production in Thirty-nine African Countries

	1961–65	1970	1980
Indigenous production per head			
Cattle	11.9 kg	10.6 kg	13.2 kg
Sheep and goats	3.3 kg	3.3 kg	3.7 kg
Indigenous production per person			
Beef and veal	6.2 kg	5.5 kg	5.6 kg
Goat meat, lamb and mutton	2.2 kg	2.2 kg	2.4 kg
Inventory per person			
Cattle	0.5 head	0.5 head	0.4 head
Sheep and goats	0.7 head	0.7 head	0.7 head

Source: Simpson 1984.

for our purpose, failure is defined as the inability of a project to meet objectives in terms of livestock productivity.

Many existing articles assign varying degrees of blame to donor agencies, government policies, poor project design, poor management, and lack of needed information. In fact, the literature is so extensive and rife with conflicting information and conclusions that one could effectively argue that there is either great hope of future success or no hope at all (Atherton 1984; Jahnke 1982), that pastoralists either do or do not degrade the range under traditional herding practices (Livingstone 1977; Lamprey 1983; Sandford 1983; McCabe 1988), or that there either are or are not a number of technical innovations appropriate for increasing livestock production in Africa's rangelands (Simpson 1984; Moris 1986).

Today, however, a consensus seems to be emerging on at least some of the development issues. For example, articles which discuss the failure of livestock development projects increasingly describe how many of these projects are plagued with conflicting policy objectives, often based on mistaken and unquestioned assumptions concerning pastoral production systems and arid land ecosystems. Another reason cited for project failures is that anthropologists have not been able to make significant contributions to the design or implementation of successful programs.

ANTHROPOLOGY AND THE DEVELOPMENT PROCESS

First-rate, prominent anthropologists who have studied pastoral peoples have been involved, to varying extents, in livestock development projects in Sub-Saharan Africa. In East Africa, Neville Dyson-Hudson, Alan Jacobs, and Gunner Haaland stand out as senior with other less senior individuals such as Johan Helland, Peter Little, and Richard Hogg also recently involved. In West Africa anthropologists such as Michael Horowitz, Jeremy Swift, and Dan Aronson immediately come to mind. In addition, a number of nonanthropologists who are very knowledgeable about pastoral peoples and appreciate the anthropological perspective have been intimately involved in development; Stephen Sandford and Jon Moris fall into this category.

In addition to prominent anthropologists involved in the region, extensive ethnographic information has already been collected for East African pastoral peoples. Following the lead of E. E. Evans-Pritchard and his classic ethnographic account of the Nuer, a number of British and American anthropologists began intensive studies of many of the East African pastoral peoples. Much of what we know today emerged from the work undertaken during this period by Dyson-Hudson among the Karamojong (1966), Gulliver among the Turkana and Jie (1955), Schneider among the Pokot (1957), Jacobs among the Maasai (1965a, 1965b), Baxter among the Borana (1975, 1979), Spencer among the Samburu (1965, 1973), and Goldschmidt among the Sebei (1967, 1976).

These ethnographic accounts have been supplemented by the more recent work of Torry (1973), Dahl (1979), Dahl and Hjort (1976), Legesse (1973), Rigby (1969), Galaty (1981), Klima (1970), and Ensminger (1984), among others. Although not an exhaustive listing of all work conducted among East African pastoral populations, this body of literature demonstrates that there is indeed a wealth of information available to development planners and implementors concerning a great many of the ethnic groups to be affected by livestock development projects.

Of course not all that is written by anthropologists is useful to development planners. Anthropological accounts in general, and those concerning nomadic pastoralists in particular, often lack the production data and economic analysis which development planners view as critical. Because many ethnographic researchers do not view the subsistence or production system as particularly relevant to their work, outsiders often view ethnographic accounts as an exercise in pure esoterica. Chambers summarizes the attitude of some "practitioners" toward academic social science as follows: "To some narrowly practical administrators and scientists, academic social scientists appear to indulge in esoteric and incestuous debate, muttering to one another in private languages" (1983:30). Raikes, speaking directly of the anthropological literature concerning East African pastoralism, says, "Much of this literature is devoted to debating problems which appear irrelevant to technicians while the language in which many of the studies are written can be dauntingly complex to outsiders. Apart from this, there is a sense in which overdetailed reporting of those symbolic aspects of daily life and social transactions which strike the observer as 'exotic' can actually detract from a coherent or convincing presentation of the systems of production" (Raikes 1981:250).

Although there is some truth to Chambers's and Raikes's accusations, there is a danger in assuming that institutions such as kinship, ritual, or religion have no relationship to the system of production (Galaty 1981; Rappaport 1984). It is not too much to expect that those engaging in livestock development gain some facility with the problems addressed by anthropologists studying pastoral peoples.

For many reasons—two principal ones—little information exists on the productivity of livestock managed under traditional conditions. First, many East African pastoralists expressly prohibit the counting of livestock or the measurement of milk. Second, the human and livestock population is often divided into separate units which change in size and composition throughout the year according to environmental conditions and the availability of labor. These groups may move independently of one another, often in opposite directions, making detailed recording of productivity extremely difficult if one is to rely on anything but survey questionnaires. I can personally attest to the difficulty presented by this combination of factors because the collection of data on livestock productivity and herd dynamics was a critical feature of the field research upon which my dissertation is based (McCabe 1985, 1987a, 1987b). Although some methodological advances are being made in this area (*see* Grandin 1983), we are still far from having an adequate data base from which we can build comparative models of livestock productions systems.

Few would deny the need for more information on pastoral production, but the extent to which the availability of more data would have influenced the design of pastoral development is questionable. A common criticism of development projects is that what is already known, even about their own failures, is often ignored. A more detailed look at livestock development policy and project design may help explain why what we already do know is often not incorporated in development planning.

A common theme of most failures in livestock development is the lack of cooperation or the subverting of project objectives by the pastoral people whom the project is intended to "benefit." This has led to castigation of pastoral people by developers in the past as well as to the feeling among some planners that anthropologists, who were supposed to be experts in these "social areas," have little to offer the projects.

Livestock development policy in East Africa has revolved around a few important considerations: first, the necessity of increasing the supply of beef either to national markets or for export; second, the preservation of rangeland resources from overexploitation and eventual degradation; third, low consumer prices if the intended outlet for beef is the national market; and fourth, the improvement of the quality of life of the pastoral population, a goal principally restricted to development rhetoric. Balancing the obvious conflicts resulting from these policy considerations is difficult, if not impossible. Michael Horowitz sums up the dilemma resulting from conflicting policy objectives as follows: "It is not easy to increase production while improving rangeland conditions, and to keep consumer prices low while improving producer income—all the while assuring an adequate return on investment. The concurrent satisfaction of these objectives never occurs" (Horowitz 1986:255).

Livestock development policy in East Africa has taken as a given that the communal ownership of land combined with the private ownership of livestock will necessarily lead to environmental degradation. This line of reasoning, commonly referred to as the "tragedy of the commons" (Hardin 1968), was attacked on theoretical grounds shortly after its publication and has been the subject of much recent debate as it relates to African pastoralists (Sandford 1983; Horowitz 1986; McCabe 1988). Nevertheless, it has been one of the cornerstones upon which livestock development policy has been constructed.

The need for increased livestock productivity, in the form of meat, combined with the assumed need to preserve the rangeland has influenced livestock development policy and the subsequent design of projects—by directing the focus of increasing productivity on individual animals (rather than increasing overall numbers) and by viewing traditional management strategies, such as frequent movements and a dependence on milk for food, as constraints to the implementation of successful livestock development projects. The view that traditional forms of social organization were obstacles to be overcome was not restricted to policymakers or technicians but also dominated much of the overall research conducted on livestock development in Africa. The International Livestock Center for Africa has been conducting development related research since its inception in 1975. Cees de Haan, quoting Nestle (the lead author of a report by a task force commissioned by the Africa Livestock Sub-committee of the Consultive Group on International Agricultural Research) outlines ILCA's strategy in approaching livestock development research: "Technical answers are available to many of the specific problems facing livestock development in Africa, but the major constraint lies in introducing change into existing socioeconomic systems" (de Haan 1983:25).

However, the real problem is not one of changing the existing socioeconomic systems only. Instead, the problem was perceived as how to transform African pastoralists into livestock producers much like ranchers found in the arid areas in North America and Australia. Individual, group, and cooperative ranches were designed—as well as grazing blocks and other schemes—which in addition to technical improvements also included the restructuring of society. Anthropologists were asked to help formulate plans and evaluate projects based on these new social units which often involved restricting access to resources in a manner completely contrary to the norms and values of the traditional society.

The importance of social rights and obligations, especially those involving the exchange of livestock, has been well documented in the anthropological literature concerning pastoral people. The literature does not give the impression that these aspects of social organization are weakly defined or easily manipulated. Yet project after project was designed on the notion that new social formations could be engineered and that project participants would adhere to the rules of the project rather than the norms of the society in which the project is imbedded.

One theoretical perspective which helps explain the desire of pastoral peoples to adhere to traditional norms and values suggests that the goal of a pastoral subsistence strategy is not the maximization of livestock but the maximization of people. There are numerous examples of pastoral social institutions and living arrangements which help families gain access to livestock following a drought, disease outbreak, or raid. Individuals may move within the family from poorer to wealthier branches during times of stress. People who leave the pastoral system during lean times, to practice agriculture or for nonagricultural employment, often return when conditions become more favorable. Dyson-Hudson refers to this as a "population strategy" because "its beneficiary is a breeding population, not an individual" (1986:178).

The benefit of hindsight suggests that pastoralists were behaving sensibly by rejecting the regulations imposed by livestock projects which required them to adopt foreign, often maladaptive behaviors. However, not all development strategies are rejected by pastoralists. For example, research conducted among the Masai has revealed that they have accepted the division of their land into group ranches because they see the ownership of land as necessary to prevent the encroachment of other ethnic groups into their traditional grazing lands (Galaty 1981; Oxby 1981) and not because they recognize these new social groupings as advantageous from the standpoint of livestock production. In other words, pastoralists are not necessarily opposed to change nor are they "conservative," but change must be perceived as in their best interests or it will not be adopted.

Determining why social scientists have not been able to help design and implement successful livestock development projects in East Africa is complex and involves such factors as traditional ethnographic field methods, the esoteric nature of some ethnographic writing, and the difficulty of collecting data on livestock productivity. Nevertheless, anthropologists have been thrust into a milieu of conflicting objectives and strategies which have been impossible to overcome. Of course, important obstacles not necessarily related to the anthropologist's role may impede the development process, such as poor project design, mismanagement, and inadequately trained staff.

The inability of social scientists to discover social solutions to livestock development has reinforced the positions of those who view development in purely technical terms. Unfortunately this position is gaining increasing acceptance in African livestock development. One example of this changing attitude is the virtual disappearance of the anthropological component in the research conducted by the International Livestock Center for Africa.

Although anthropologists were incorporated into ILCA's research design, they were principally used to describe existing systems or help train others to collect interview data. Barbara Grandin worked for a number of years in the early and mid-1980s on ICLA's Kenya program and has stated quite clearly how she views the role that anthropologists have had in the International Agricultural Research Centers (IARC) to which ILCA belongs: "NSS (non economic social scientists) act largely in a service capacity: (1) to biological scientists who are perceived as doing the "real work" (i.e., technology development), and (2) to the economic scientists who are thought to do the "real evaluation" (i.e., neo-classical cost-benefit analysis)" (Grandin 1986:4). However, anthropologists have made significant contributions to some of the other IARC programs, in particular that of the International Potato Center (CIP), located in Lima, Peru. Anthropologists associated with CIP have been particularly successful in improving postharvest technology (Rhodes 1984) and helping geneticists understand the needs of local farmers in their plant breeding programs (Haugarud 1988). Moreover, they have been instrumental in incorporating farmers into the development process itself—the "farmer back to farmer" approach.

Unfortunately, it does not appear that anthropologists working in livestock development can model their work after the successful program at CIP. Attempts to improve livestock productivity through breeding programs have enjoyed limited success, and little attention has been paid to postharvest technology. Pastoral participation has proved difficult because of the mobility of the population and a general distrust in government sponsored programs (*see* Sandford 1983 for more detail). The net result has been the curtailment of the anthropological component on the one hand and the retreat of donor agencies and research organizations from programs designed to improve livestock production in Africa's arid zones on the other (ILCA is phasing out its commitment to arid zone research [ILCA 1987]).

WHERE NOW?

There is a growing sense of resignation and impotence among those who have been involved in livestock development in Sub-Saharan Africa. Recent statements by both Moris and Jahnke reflect this attitude:

> Of course range scientists can use the implicit notion of controlled stocking rates to defend the supposed benefits to be realized from group ranches, just as sociologists can argue for the need to give producers a voice in their own development. The fact is, however, that the formation of viable group organizations among pastoralists requires an enormous input of liaison and reeducation. Until there are at least a few examples of enduring, economically successful units, it would seem rash indeed to expect the new units will have any better record than those formed in the past. . . . Maybe it would be cheaper to issue the heads of compounds with barbed wire, and let them settle the matter their own way. (Moris 1986:5, 6)

> Human rather than livestock development is the task in the arid zones. The livestock production system can only marginally be improved upon, and from a certain degree of aridity onwards the migratory form of land use through livestock is the most efficient. Human development does not mean teaching pastoralists better methods of stock raising, but making them fit for the occupation in other zones and sectors. (Jahnke 1982:103)

Although the constraints to livestock development appear to be insurmountable, the results of recent research suggest that a development paradigm based on the existing system of livestock management is worth investigating.[4] The efficiency of pastoral production systems, the willingness of pastoralists to sell livestock, and recent findings concerning the nature of arid land ecosystems are addressed in Behnke (1985), Evangelou (1984), Horowitz (1981), Meadows and White (1979), and Ellis and Swift (1988).

Behnke (1985) has very effectively argued that the comparison of productivity made between livestock raised on experimental ranches and those raised in traditional pastoral herds cannot be used to evaluate overall system productivity. Using data collected by Meadows and

White (1979) for the Kenyan Maasai, Behnke concludes that "The more closely and accurately the gap between subsistence and commercial production is quantified, it would appear, the more the two systems seem to achieve rough economic parity" (Behnke 1985:128).

Behnke points out that subsistence production has been both underestimated and undervalued. Where the commercial systems which the development planners are trying to operationalize are no more productive than the traditional systems, efforts to improve the efficiency of the traditional systems may yield some positive results.

A commonly held assumption has been that pastoralists have been unwilling to sell stock and that the typical patterns of sales suggests economic irrationality. To the contrary, recent studies suggest that the principal constraint to pastoral participation in the national economy relates far more to policy decisions concerning the marketing of livestock than some inherent lack of desire on the part of the pastoralists to part with their livestock (Evangelou 1984; Horowitz 1981; Meadows and White 1979).

Not enough attention has been given to creating the proper environment and incentives for pastoralists to market livestock. Pastoralists will market livestock when it is in their best interests to do so. Livestock markets need to be reliable, flexible enough to withstand the periodicities characteristic of pastoral production systems, and equitable in providing a rate of return superior to that provided by keeping the animal.

Existing literature strongly suggests that it is possible to increase the number of animals per unit of rangeland with the provision of increased water availability and veterinary services. Doing so, of course, is the recipe for disaster if the livestock cannot be removed from the range— especially true in times of drought when the livestock population will greatly exceed range carrying capacity, as documented for the Sahelian drought (Picardi and Siefert 1976; Sinclair and Fryxell 1985). However, if the constraint to marketing livestock from traditional production systems is principally a policy issue rather than one of pastoral ideology, then an increase in the livestock population may not necessarily lead to an environmental disaster.

Finally, some of the results of the South Turkana Ecosystem Project challenge the generally accepted ecological paradigm that pastoral ecosystems in Africa's arid lands function according to principals of equilibrium. According to the equilibrium paradigm, a pastoral ecosystem is regulated by density dependent relationships among livestock species and vegetation. Thus an expansion of the livestock population will lead to overgrazing and environmental degradation. The solution to this problem is to reduce the livestock population so that the ecosystem can be restored to a balanced state. However, Ellis and Swift have recently argued that these systems are persistent, but not equilibrial, and that system dynamics are controlled by abiotic (especially droughts) rather than by biotic factors (1988). If these ecosystems are not stable systems to begin with, attempts to limit livestock numbers will be ineffectual to restore the system to an assumed healthy condition.

The consensus which emerges from the literature is threefold: (1) livestock development projects predicated on the notion that pastoral social organization is an inappropriate framework for development have failed, (2) many projects are plagued with conflicting goals and poorly defined policy objectives, and (3) enough evidence may have been accumulated to influence development planners to jettison ideas of restructuring pastoral society as a necessary first step in livestock development.

The literature also reveals that anthropologists have not been able to influence policymakers and development planners to orient development projects to address the needs and desires of the pastoral people themselves, despite repeated calls for such an orientation (Hoben 1979; Galaty et al. 1981).

It seems rather trite to state that anthropologists must be able to participate fully in livestock development and not be relegated to a service capacity. It also seems trite to join the chorus calling for pastoral involvement in the development process. Nevertheless, until pastoralists themselves are committed to the development of the livestock industry, there is no reason to think that livestock production in Africa's arid lands will show any marked increase. Anthropologists familiar with pastoral people are better suited than other scientists (natural or social) to help design development projects which put the pastoralists' interests ahead of, or at least on a par with, the interests of planners. Those who make policy decisions and those who plan development must give serious attention to projects that involve pastoralists in their own development and in which the real beneficiary is the livestock producer.

Until this change occurs the current trend of repeated failures is likely
to continue.

NOTES

I want to thank Tom Reardon (IFPRI) and David Brokensha (IDA), who
commented on earlier drafts of this paper.

1. A more commonly cited figure for international donor expenditures for
livestock development in Sub-Saharan Africa is $600 million for the period
1965–80.

2. Much of what is related here and in the following section is based on the
work of Raikes (1981) and Migot-Adholla and Little (1981).

3. Although the term *carrying capacity* has proved difficult to define in
the East African Rangeland context, it generally refers to the number of animals which can exploit the rangeland resources without causing environmental
degradation. In the Turkana context, we have used the term to mean the number of animals which will consume less than 50 percent of the net primary
production during a given year (Coughenour et al. 1985).

4. The idea of basing livestock development projects upon existing forms
of pastoral social organization is certainly not new (*see* Hoben 1979) but has
yet to be seriously considered for East Africa.

Anthropology and the Analysis of African Food Markets: Assessing Market Efficiency at the Village Level

Edward B. Reeves

Market efficiency—the conditions that must be met for goods to be moved from producers to consumers at lowest cost—has emerged as a central problem in food policy analysis (Gittinger, Leslie, and Hoisington 1987; Timmer, Falcon, and Pearson 1983). Economists have developed two basic techniques for assessing market efficiency: market margin analysis and price analysis. Market margin analysis deals with estimated costs of such factors as transportation, storage, and the profit margins of middlemen. Price analysis, on the other hand, focuses on price movements in regional markets to determine how well integrated the system of markets is.

The usefulness of both market margin analysis and price analysis depends on the accuracy of the data that is fed into the analysis. Faulty data and rough estimates may lead to results that would seriously mislead policymakers. Under rural conditions in Africa, appropriate and accurate information for these kinds of analyses can be difficult to acquire. Therefore, food policy analysts must seek additional sources of information for estimating market efficiency. One of the contributions which anthropologists can make to food policy analysis is to supplement the economist's tools of market analysis by gathering data on how markets actually work, who the participants are, and how they acquire working capital and information about prices. This type of research can provide governments with more accurate information on market organization and help them design more effective policies to relieve areas of actual or projected market inefficiency which functions as a constraint on total food production and consumption.

A study of village crop assemblers or middlemen in thirteen villages in North Kordofan, Sudan, demonstrates the utility of anthropological research techniques to complement the sorts of measures that would ordinarily be used to assess market efficiency. The research was conducted over a thirteen-month period in 1981–82 as part of the University of Kentucky/International Sorghum-Millet (INTSORMIL) Research Project's farming systems study in North Kordofan (Reeves and Frakenberger 1981, 1982; Reeves 1984; Coughenour and Nazhat 1985; Coughenour and Reeves 1989).

This chapter is divided into five main sections:

1. a review of the concept of market efficiency—what economists mean by it and the techniques that have been developed to measure it—followed by a discussion of some of the shortcomings of these techniques when applied to contemporary African food markets;
2. a description of the el-Obeid marketing system and the numerous channels through which food commodities pass from producers' fields to urban warehousers and processors;
3. a discussion of the complex role of the village crop assembler and the close relationship between crop buying and providing credit to agricultural producers;
4. a quantitative analysis of market efficiency which studies the effect village conditions have on the crop assembler's use of four kinds of marketing channels—rural auctions, rural agents, urban auctions, and urban merchants;
5. a review of the implications of this research for food policy analysis, including how it may complement or correct shortcomings in measures of market efficiency derived from market margin analysis and price analysis.

BACKGROUND: THE CONCEPT OF MARKET EFFICIENCY AND AFRICAN FOOD MARKETS

Economic Techniques for Measuring Market Efficiency

Neoclassical economics identifies five conditions for an efficient market to exist (Timmer, Falcon, and Pearson 1983:165–66):

1. *Fungible and divisible commodities.* Are the commodities fungible (interchangeable) and divisible?
2. *Economically rational buyers and sellers.* Do buyers and sellers act in an economically rational way (want more, and not less, of incomes and goods)?
3. *Competitiveness.* Are firms small and numerous so that the decisions of any one firm or a small number of firms have no impact on prices?
4. *Unrestricted market entry.* Do all participants have equal access to activities of the market on the same terms?
5. *Full and unrestricted information.* Does everyone have complete knowledge of forces likely to influence supply and demand?

While the presence of all of these conditions may produce an efficient marketing system, they need not be fully realized for a reasonably competitive market to exist. In fact, efficient markets may exist as long as market information and relatively unrestricted access are present and a few large firms do not have the ability to manipulate prices.

Generally in African food markets, commodities are fungible and divisible, and market participants, whether producers or middlemen, respond rationally to price signals. Therefore, economists focus on the issues of market competitiveness, entry, and information. However, economists have difficulty collecting survey data to determine whether the marketing system is operating under circumstances that approximate the competitive ideal of neoclassical economics closely enough. Because of the expense and difficulty of getting quality survey data under African field conditions, economists have preferred to use two indirect methods of determining market efficiency: market margin analysis and price analysis.

Market Margin Analysis

Market margin analysis looks at the spread between producer prices and consumer (or urban wholesale) prices. A large spread in prices, or marketing margin, can be an indication either of technical shortcomings in marketing or of a lack of competition. In the first instance, high real marketing costs—such as transport, storage, and processing costs—may explain why consumer prices are much higher than producer prices. In the second instance, monopolistic elements, poor information, and barriers to market entry can account for large market margin disparity. Thus, by analyzing marketing costs, economists can discover which set of factors is most responsible when high market margins exist. In calculating this, the net profit of rural middlemen, for example, should not exceed the interest rate for capital, after the costs of storage, transportation, and processing are deducted from gross earnings. The interest rate for capital is equated with the cost of the middleman's entrepreneurship.

Price Analysis

Price analysis, the second indirect method for assessing market efficiency, is based on the assumption that an efficient marketing system will reveal relatively high correlation coefficients between price movements at different marketing centers. In other words, a rising trend in prices at one center will be answered by a similar trend in other centers. Economists account for this phenomenon by noting that in an efficient marketing system where price information and capital are well-distributed, commodities will tend to move from areas of excess supply to areas of scarcity rather quickly because of arbitrage (buying in one market to sell in another). As a result, the price at point B should be about the same as the price at point A minus transportation costs.

Difficulties of Applying Market Margin Analysis and
Price Analysis in the African Context

Timmer, Falcon, and Pearson (1983) advise that because of the rigorous data requirements of market margin analysis and the often poor quality of price data available for price analysis, these methods should be used jointly to ascertain market efficiency whenever possible. Used in tandem, market margin analysis and price analysis are powerful tools for assessing market efficiency and for informing food policy; however, shortcomings of these approaches are particularly acute in the African context. These shortcomings point to a strong need for local studies of market behavior to supplement these techniques.

The difficulties of basing food policy in African countries solely on the findings of market margin analysis and price analysis are several:

1. In African countries, the price and commodity data in official records is often seriously flawed (Hill 1986). The records may contain large gaps as well as inaccuracies. Data may not be recorded consistently or conscientiously, and deliberate falsification of records is not unknown.

2. Market margin analysis looks at the costs added with each stage of exchange or processing as the commodity is moved from producer to consumer. The data requirements of this approach are stringent and make it necessary for the analyst to estimate *average* costs for transport, storage, processing, and entrepreneurship. Such estimations may be difficult to come by under typical field conditions in Africa. Moreover, averages can mask local variation and disturb the results. Using estimations of average costs means assuming that real cost values are normally distributed. But if village conditions affecting entrepreneurship, storage, processing, and transportation are not normally distributed, real cost values will be skewed and estimates of averages will not reflect this variation.

3. Estimating the interest rate of capital, given that it is likely to vary according to season, locality, and even the social identity of creditor and borrower, is especially problematic, a fact that makes the matter of determining acceptable market margins for middlemen a judgment call at best. Factoring such judgment calls into the analysis of market margins as if they were hard data must be viewed with extreme caution.

4. Price analysis has been used most often to look at the integration of major regional markets and may be used to infer wrongly that prices in these bellwether markets are transmitted to village markets undistorted (Harriss 1979a, 1979b).

5. When using these techniques, economists sometimes overlook the competitiveness of markets at the village level since to explore this issue extensively with either the market margin approach or the price integration approach would entail substantial research expenditures.[1]

The need for village-level studies of market behavior which can supplement the economic methods of assessing efficiency and competitiveness is apparent. In this paper I describe an anthropological field study that collected data on village markets and rural participants in food marketing networks. The study was able to shed light on how village-level conditions affect the efficiency of the el-Obeid marketing system in North Kordofan, Sudan. The research took aim at assessing market entry and access to information, which I have noted are important issues in neoclassical economic definition of market efficiency.

Among the factors considered were the availability of working capital, the availability of secure storage, the number of shopkeeper/crop assemblers in the village (a measure of local competition), the number of market trucks in the village, and whether a government-administered crop auction is present (another indicator of competition as well as information flow). Significant variation between villages along these dimensions could be interpreted as signs of village-level market inefficiencies. In assessing how marketing choices are affected by village-level conditions such as these, the analysis should deal comprehensively with the different types of actors in the marketing chain (e.g., agricultural producers as opposed to rural middlemen). For purposes of illustration, the present paper deals with the marketing choices of village crop assemblers in the el-Obeid marketing system.

The techniques described are not offered as polished research tools but as a stimulus for economic anthropologists to think about research methods that could be relevant for food policy analysis.

EL-OBEID FOOD CROP MARKETING SYSTEM

Field research was carried out in 1981–82 by the INTSORMIL/ University of Kentucky Farming Systems Research Project of which the author was field director.[2] The main thrust of the study was to focus on the farming systems of limited-resource agriculturalists in the el-Obeid area. This involved surveys of approximately 150 producer households regarding their agricultural enterprises, livestock, and off-farm employment. A household consumption survey was also made of 25 rural households. A secondary thrust of the study was to analyze the village-level food marketing system. Initially, we performed rapid surveys of eighteen villages in el-Obeid marketing region to determine their economic and institutional characteristics, including factors reported in this article such as the number of secure storage buildings, number of village assemblers/shopkeepers, number of market trucks, and presence of a government-administered crop auction. In April and May 1982 (the end of the crop buying season), we then performed a survey of 58 shopkeepers in thirteen of the original eighteen villages. These villages were selected to represent a wide range of institutional and economic characteristics.

The shopkeepers that were surveyed comprised a 50-percent, random sample in each village. Forty-five of the 58 shopkeepers had been active in crop assembling that year. This group is the basis for the quantitative analysis in the fifth section below.

We interviewed the village assemblers/shopkeepers to learn what crops were purchased from producers and in what quantities and how these same commodities were sold to other rural middlemen or to urban buyers. This information gave us a comprehensive picture of the crop assembler's role in the market. In addition, we sought information about the personal characteristics of village assemblers and their different enterprises.

The field research was carried out during a low-average year (1981–82) of rainfall and crop production.[3]

Overview of el-Obeid Marketing System

El-Obeid (Figure 1) has been the major marketing center in Kordofan since it was settled by Dongolawi traders from northern Sudan about 1750. However, its modern character as an entrepot with a large agricultural hinterland is a result of twentieth-century developments. The town was made a colonial administrative center in 1912 and became a regional capital after independence in 1956. Steady growth of the urban population in recent decades has created a high level of consumer food demand—satisfied in part by the region's local agricultural production.

Agriculture in this semiarid region combines sorghum and millet production, staples primarily consumed within the villages, with the production of sesame, groundnut, roselle, and watermelon for sale. *Acacia senegal,* a native of the region's sandy soils, produces gum arabic, an important cash crop that is harvested during the dry season. While nearly all the sesame grown in the el-Obeid area is consumed in the area, gum arabic, which is almost exclusively grown as an export crop, and significant portions of groundnut, roselle, and water-

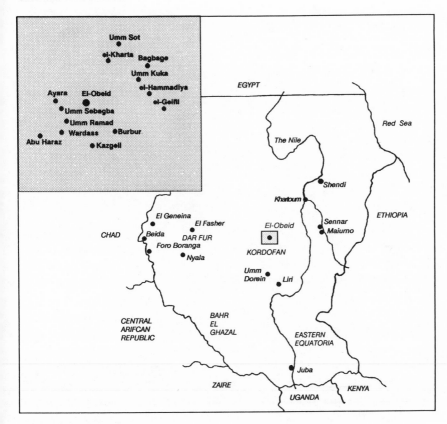

Figure 1
El-Obeid Marketing Area

melon seed are exported. Producers of these crops also diversify by raising cattle, sheep, and goats. In addition, nearly every agricultural family supplements its income through dry-season enterprises such as migratory labor, itinerant trading, charcoal making, hauling water, or operating a village shop.

A common marketing system has developed for moving food crops produced for sale (groundnut, roselle, sesame, and watermelon seed) from rural producers to urban processors, warehousers, and consumers (Figure 2). Producers may sell crops in five different channels: the government-administered urban auction at el-Obeid, the village crop assembler, the government-administered rural auction, the rural agent

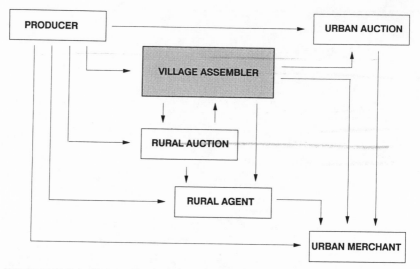

Note: Does not include millet and sorghum since these crops are typically
consumed in the producer's household or exchanged during local ceremonies.

Figure 2
The Marketing System for el-Obeid Area

(usually a transporter who buys crops on commission for an urban merchant), and directly to the urban merchant (a processor or warehouser).
The village assembler, who buys directly either from producers or from
the rural auction, has the option of selling in four different channels: the
urban auction, the rural auction, to a rural agent, or directly to an urban
merchant.

Sesame, groundnut, roselle, watermelon seed, and gum arabic are
moved alike through all the channels (Figure 2). Millet and sorghum
may also be marketed through some of the channels in this system
but never at the government-sponsored rural or urban auctions. Since
food grains are grown primarily for household consumption and surpluses are given away in social exchange between the villagers, the
locally produced food grains do not enter the marketing system in significant quantities. Massive quantities of sorghum are imported into the
el-Obeid area from mechanized farming schemes in South Kordofan
and White Nile Regions. The distribution of this grain is through a
different marketing system than the one described here.

Marketing Season, Transportation, and Storage

The marketing season begins in late October at the end of the rainy season when most crops are harvested and roads are passable by truck. The season continues until April or May, although the busiest period is from November until February. Crop prices typically begin to rise in November, reaching their highest point in February and then slightly declining until the very end of the marketing season when there may be a sudden spurt in prices which clears the market.

Bulk transport is provided by *suq* lorries, large flatbed trucks. Some villages have one or more truck owners in residence, greatly facilitating transport of crops for persons in the village. Otherwise, a village must depend on periodic visits from transporters to haul crops. Camel, donkey, or horse-drawn cart transport is used for short distances, for example, from field to storehouse and from storehouse to rural auction.

Storage of modest amounts of crops is often in unoccupied space in thatched huts, although fire and theft are hazards. Secure storage for some months is accomplished by filling underground pits, but this method of storage does not permit easy access. Accessible bulk storage which the village crop assemblers require is best facilitated by adobe or brick structures; however, these are not available in every village.

The Principal Players

The Producer. Agriculturalists in the el-Obeid area must make a choice between investing their limited labor to produce cereal grains for household consumption or marketable food crops such as sesame, groundnut, roselle, and watermelon seed. Generally, the higher the ratio of working adults within the household the more labor is devoted to producing cash crops rather than cereal grains. Conversely, when there are more mouths to feed than working adults in the household, more labor is allocated to growing millet and sorghum. However, nearly all households produce some mix of these cereal grains.

Local producers vary enormously in terms of the amount of working capital they have at their disposal and the size of the family labor force. In general, however, most farm families grow a high ratio of cash to subsistence food crops. Family subsistence food needs are then supplemented with purchases of grain produced outside the region.

The Village Crop Assembler. The marketing system hinges on the activities of village assemblers who buy food crops from producers and sell them to merchant's agents working in the rural areas or more directly to wholesalers and processors in el-Obeid. These structurally key middlemen are invariably diversified into other enterprises, mainly agricultural production and shopkeeping. The critical role of the village assembler is discussed in more detail later in this chapter.

The Rural Agent. The rural agent buys crops in bulk for an urban merchant. Often he receives cash advances from the merchant to make these purchases and is awarded a commission when the crops are delivered to the merchant's warehouse in el-Obeid. Rural agents are typically truck owners themselves or related to truck owners.

The Rural Auction. Five of the villages in the study have a rural auction administered by a clerk appointed by the Peoples' Rural Council, headquartered at el-Obeid. The rural auction is convened only once or twice a week, depending on the volume of crops to be sold. The clerk's role is to administer the auctioning of crops and to record all transactions, including the amount of taxes assessed from the buyer. Two kinds of taxes are assessed, *'ushur* and *gibana.* The most important tax is *'ushur,* which is a 15 percent ad valorem tax assessed on the total price given for the total amount of crops sold at auction. *Gibana* is a much lower market use tax. The clerk's final duty is to collect and hold tax monies until they are picked up by an official from the Rural Council headquarters. These taxes are the primary source of Rural Council revenues in the el-Obeid area.

The rural auction allows producers and some village assemblers to sell sizeable quantities of crops to buyers who bid competitively. Generally, the prices obtained at the rural auctions approximate the current daily prices at the el-Obeid urban auction less sacking, handling, and transportation costs. Thus, the rural auctions are an important source of price information for the rural population.

The Urban Auction. The urban auction at el-Obeid is the central assembly point for the sesame, groundnut, roselle, watermelon seed, and gum arabic that are produced in the region. Similar to the rural auction, the urban auction allows the *'ushur* and *gibana* taxes to be collected, and it is overseen by a market officer and several deputies. In contrast to the rural auction, the urban auction takes place daily except Fridays. To bid at the auction and buy crops, one must obtain a permit from

the el-Obeid District Council. The buyers at the urban auction are merchants from el-Obeid as well as representatives of export firms located
in Khartoum and Port Sudan.

The Urban Merchant. There are approximately two dozen players
in this group who reside in el-Obeid. They are the main wholesale
buyers of all of the sesame, groundnut, roselle, watermelon seed, and
gum arabic that is produced in the area. In addition to crop buying,
their extensive enterprises may include warehousing, oilseed milling,
long distance transport, and mechanized sorghum production in South
Kordofan. Often the urban merchant at el-Obeid acts in part as an agent
for export firms based in Khartoum and Port Sudan.

Marketing Options at the Village Level

To illustrate how the el-Obeid marketing system works at the village
level, I will compare the marketing options of producers and village assemblers (Figure 2). The discussion will show that different constraints
and opportunities determine which channel(s) an actor chooses. First,
we consider the options of the producer.

1. *Producer sells at urban auction.* Typically, this option is most
   available to large producers who can attract the services of a
   truck operator. On the other hand, small producers sometimes
   pool their crops for the same purpose. The higher prices that
   urban auction generally brings make this a preferred channel of
   sale. Prices are somewhat higher than rural prices even taking
   the increased handling and transportation costs into account. In
   addition, the producer has the opportunity to buy supplies while
   in el-Obeid with his earnings.
2. *Producer sells to village assembler.* The producer trades small
   quantities of crops to obtain commodities from the crop assembler's shop. This marketing strategy is important for most producers early in the marketing season when the prices for crops
   are still low. Essentially, producers are using crops as a substitute
   for cash. For poorer producers whose yields have not been good,
   this system may be their only means of marketing crops.
3. *Producer sells at rural auction.* Small producers who are able to
   hold back substantial portions of crops rather than trade them to

the village assembler for food and supplies may sell in this channel. Prices are not as good as when selling to a rural agent or in
one of the urban channels, but the competition of the auction will
bring better prices than direct sales to a village assembler. This
marketing opportunity is often the best one for small producers.

4. *Producer sells to rural agent.* Direct sales by producers to rural
agents operating trucks and buying crops on commission for urban
merchants occur most often late in the marketing season (March
through May). At this time producers open their storage pits before the onset of the rains and sell the remainder of their crops to
pay for land clearing and to buy sorghum while the price of this
essential food commodity is still low (sorghum prices are generally highest during the rainy season). Truck operating agents haul
sorghum to the villages to make a direct exchange of sorghum
for the producers' crops, primarily sesame during this time of
year. To sweeten the deal, rural agents typically provide sacks
and labor for sacking and loading. The agreement to buy from
producers in this manner is always made ahead of time so that the
agent is assured of filling his truck.

Generally speaking, only large producers are able to take advantage of this channel, although small producers may pool their
crops with that of a larger producer. It should be noted that this
channel of sale typically involves tax evasion. For this reason, the
price the producer receives will be better than what he could get
at the rural auction.

5. *Producer sells to urban merchant.* Direct sale by producers to
an urban merchant is illegal since crops do not pass through
a government-administered auction where taxes are assessed.
Nevertheless, large producers who have access to a truck may
sell in this channel. According to informants, the producer, the
urban merchant, and the truck operator share in the money saved
by avoiding the *'ushur* and *gibana* taxes. The government attempts to discourage tax evasion by monitoring trucks as they
enter el-Obeid, but enforcement is spotty at best.

The options available to agricultural producers illustrate that producers' marketing options are influenced by the amounts of crops they
have to sell. Large producers can generally make use of the channels
which bring higher prices; the options available to small producers

are less advantageous. The marketing options of the village assembler present their own constraints and opportunities:

1. *Village assembler sells at urban auction.* As with the producers, the higher prices at the urban market make this the preferred legal channel for village assemblers. However, not all village assemblers can make use of it since a lack of cash (working capital) prevents many assemblers from dealing in high volumes of crops. In many cases, small assemblers, like the small producers, are compelled to sell in less advantageous channels.

2. *Village assembler sells to urban merchant.* Direct sale of crops by the crop assembler to an urban merchant in el-Obeid typically avoids taxation and brings the most rewarding prices. This marketing strategy is available only to the largest crop assemblers who have access to a truck and are willing to take the risk of having their crops confiscated for tax evasion. No large assembler would attempt to market exclusively in this channel, however. Instead, illegal crop sales are mixed with legal sales at the urban auction in order to confuse the authorities.

3. *Village assembler sells at rural auction.* This option is especially attractive to small crop assemblers who cannot always command transportation to the urban market. If large dealers, such as rural agents buying for urban merchants, are bidding at the rural auction, then prices will approximate those of the urban auction less handling and transportation costs.

4. *Village assembler sells to rural agent.* When there is not a rural auction in the village, crop assemblers may establish an agreement with a truck operator to buy large quantities of crops which the crop assemblers have accumulated over a period of weeks. The disparity between urban market prices and those in the villages provide the rural agent's profit margin. Also, since taxes are avoided by selling directly to the rural agent, profits are higher. Small assemblers often mix sales to rural agents with sales at a rural auction to optimize their profits and maintain the cash flow needed for future crop purchases as well as for replenishing the inventory of their shops.

Just as the agricultural producer's options depend on the quantity of crops he has for sale, the assembler's marketing options are limited by his amount of working capital—the cash necessary for buying, sacking, handling, and transporting food crops. Village assemblers with larger working capital may face a different set of constraints and opportunities than those with less working capital. Other factors that may influence the village assembler's marketing choices include access to motor transportation, presence of a rural auction, availability of secure storage (permitting the assembler to hold crops in volume while waiting for advantageous prices), and possibly the competition which the village assembler faces from others in the village.

THE CRITICAL ROLE OF THE VILLAGE CROP ASSEMBLER/SHOPKEEPER IN THE EL-OBEID MARKETING SYSTEM

In the survey of fifty-eight shopkeepers in thirteen villages, fifty-two were found to be agricultural producers and forty-five bought and sold food crops that were locally produced. In a couple of instances, crop assemblers were identified who did not own a shop, but these examples are unusual since crop assembling and shopkeeping are symbiotic enterprises.

All shopkeepers in the sample were males. Women are frequently vendors in periodic village markets and beer brewers, but we did not encounter a single instance in which a woman owned or operated a shop in a village. Most shopkeepers appear to take up their occupation in their twenties. Fifty-seven percent of the sample stated that agricultural success (including livestock raising) provided the starting capital for opening their shops. Another 28 percent went into business in partnership with someone else, usually a relative, who provided the start-up capital; of these, one-third inherited the business from their fathers. Itinerant retailing (7 percent), crop dealing (5 percent), and wages and separation pay for government service or work abroad (3 percent) constituted the remaining important sources of start-up capital.

Shopkeeping and Agriculture Success

Shopkeeping is generally associated with financial security and agricultural success. Shopkeepers' cultivations are approximately one-third larger than those of ordinary producers. Moreover, the shopkeeper is in a better position than the typical producer to hire additional labor during the cropping season. The survey also indicated that shopkeepers are more likely than ordinary farmers to plant a speculation crop, like groundnut. In many cases, shopkeeping served as a hedge against crop failure. Shopkeepers also stand out among producers as successful live-stock owners. They not only have larger herds but are able to invest in higher-valued animals such as cattle and sheep instead of goats. At the most basic level, shopkeeping provides the proprietor and his family with a solution to the problem which all rural families face—how to have reliable access to cash and food.

The Shop

The shop is constructed of corrugated millet thatching, adobe, or corrugated metal sheeting, depending on the owner's prosperity. A list of basic equipment for a shop would include a balance with authorized weights, a table, shelves, trays, boxes, and sacks for holding goods to be sold. Many shopkeepers build a thatched shelter next to the shop for the convenience of customers who want to loiter and talk. The shop is a major social nexus in any village, and it is not unusual to find a small group of men and boys gathered in front of it throughout the day and early evening.

Shops are usually open every day unless the shopkeeper has business that draws him away from the village. Even then, a son or some other male relative may stand in for the shopowner. Thus, the shopowner tries to maximize sales by being open as much as possible, especially during the postharvest season.

All shopkeepers sell items that are in daily demand by rural families, particularly food stuffs and common household and toilet goods. The most common commodities are tea, coffee beans, sugar, salt, red and black pepper, a dozen or so kinds of spice, dried tomatoes, canned tomato paste, biscuits, sorghum, wheat flour, yeast, onions, dried okra, pasta, sesame oil, candy, chewing gum, matches, hand soap, laundry soap, bleach, razor blades, flashlight batteries, padlocks, henna (a dye applied to the hands and feet of newlyweds and married women), kerosene, bicarbonate of soda, aspirin, chloroquine phosphate ampules (for malaria), and custard mix (for treating diarrhea in children). While most shopkeepers will have all of these commodities on hand, the availability of sorghum, wheat flour, and sugar is highly sensitive to extraregional supply networks. During the postharvest season, when customers are most likely to have cash to spend, bolts of cloth and inexpensive shoes are added to the inventory.

The goods sold in the shop are purchased from the wholesale market in el-Obeid. When supplies are purchased from a wholesaler, the shopowner or a relative must accompany the truck, buy the goods, supervise the loading, and accompany the merchandise back to the village. In some cases, the shopkeeper may make an arrangement with a truck driver to handle this task. Some of the largest shopkeepers receive credit from the wholesale distributors, but this practice is not widespread.

The Clientele

To be successful a shopkeeper must cultivate a large and loyal clientele. Relatives and friends are the core of this group. Perhaps the most important way of expanding the size of the clientele is to offer good customers credit on the supplies that they buy. Shopkeepers make credit sales to customers on a daily basis. Loaning money to trustworthy customers is also important although it does not occur as often as credit sales and affects a much smaller segment of the clientele.

Village households buy most of their purchased food (condiments, sorghum, wheat flour, sugar, tea, and vegetables) from the shopkeeper. Purchases are made daily or every few days. In 1981–82 the daily food bill ranged between 1.500 and 2.500 L.S. for the average rural family in the study.[4] Water is readily available and usually free for the taking during the rainy season (July through October); however, during the hot, dry season (March through June), in most villages water is obtained at a cost ranging as high as 0.300 L.S. per tin (about 4 gallons), and a family may need four tins per day. Since food and water have market-determined prices, a major preoccupation of village households is having sufficient cash to purchase these daily necessities.

While selling crops is a major way in which producers get money, selling immediately after the harvest poses a disadvantage. Prices are lower at this time than later in the season. Therefore, producers prefer to hold as much of their crops as they can off the market for a month or more. Shopkeepers play a major role at this point. They will accept crops in lieu of cash for purchase of goods, so the household head (or, more likely, his wife or child) sells crops in small amounts to purchase household supplies. This strategy allows the family to hold back selling crops in bulk, anticipating the rise in prices.

Starting during the dry season and continuing until the harvest, village families face another cash flow problem. Poor families and those with bad harvests the previous year will run short of crops with which to obtain cash for food and water. To some extent, the cash shortage is eased by selling labor or by taking up a seasonal trade. Nevertheless, many families experience a squeeze because household expenditures increase during the dry season as water becomes more scarce and costly. In the rainy season which follows, food costs (particularly cereal grains) are high, and there are the additional costs of agricultural inputs, especially seed and labor. Again, it is the village shopkeeper who relieves the strain by extending credit on goods purchased from his shop.[5]

Typically, credit sales entail a promise to pay back either in cash or in an amount of crops that have an equivalent value at harvest time. In the first instance, the shopkeeper may overvalue the commodity somewhat—in effect charging a flat interest rate of, say, 10 percent for a loan extending perhaps two months.[6] On the other hand, when credit is repaid in crops—which is often the case—the borrower agrees to pay after the harvest. The village assembler recoups the interest charge by holding the crops for two or more months, at which time the crops have increased in value by 20 percent.

Village Assemblers' Reputations

We often encountered government officials and others who spoke disparagingly of the shopkeeper and village assembler. In other areas of Africa as well, the rural middleman has been maligned as a monopolist and exploiter of the rural population. However, the findings of this study do not substantiate this view. Competition is assured in most villages by the presence of more than one resident shopkeeper. Furthermore, shopkeepers are usually of the same ethnic and tribal affiliation as their clienteles and that relationship lessens the potential of shopowner/ client exploitation. Village shopkeepers are key role players in the rural economy, and village families are highly dependent on their services. Moreover, nearly all shopkeepers are themselves agricultural producers as well as long-term residents in their communities.

The shopkeepers provide three important services. First, they sell a variety of consumer goods in their shops for which other villagers have a daily demand. Second, they provide consumer credit during the dry season and the cropping season. Third, and this is our primary interest here, they are the first-line assemblers of crops. As we have seen, these three roles are highly interrelated.

The ethnographic materials presented above speak strongly of a marketing system that is both flexible and competitive. Collusion, exploitation, and barriers to entry do not appear to be serious problems. Marketing efficiency also can be considered from the perspective of the village crop assembler, employing a quantitative methodology based on the survey research.

AN ANALYSIS OF FACTORS WHICH AFFECT THE USE OF MARKETING CHANNELS BY CROP ASSEMBLERS

The analysis that follows assumes that village-level market efficiency can be gauged at least in part by determining if conditions which pertain to different villages constrain the marketing choices of village assemblers. If numerous constraints exist, then village assemblers do not have freedom of access to different marketing channels and the marketing system is inefficient. Moreover, knowledge of urban prices may be restricted if village conditions do not permit ready access to a rural auction. Therefore, the options which the village assembler faces illustrate efficiencies or constraints in the overall marketing system.

As already noted, village assemblers have a choice of four marketing channels in which to sell crops purchased from agricultural producers. According to the findings of the survey, 71 percent of the village assemblers sold crops at the urban auction, 27 percent sold to an urban merchant, 31 percent sold at a rural auction, and 33 percent sold to a rural agent. Also, 48 percent of the village assemblers sold in more than one channel during the 1981–82 season. In the analysis below, we will consider whether village-level conditions affected entry to any of the above channels. We will also explore whether village-level conditions

Table 1

Probit Analysis of the Effects of Village-Level Conditions on the Use of Crop Market Channels by Village Assemblers (N = 45)

	Use of Crop Market Channels				
	Rural Auction	Rural Agent	Urban Auction	Urban Merchant	More Than One Channel
Village-level conditions					
Working capital	−.776[a]	−.631	.726[a]	1.080[a]	.241
	(.345)	(.329)	(.329)	(.417)	(.276)
No. of storage buildings	−.137	−.209	−.502	.961	.029
	(.223)	(.219)	(.452)	(1.442)	(.214)
No. of shopkeepers	−1.252	1.041	3.299	−3.860	−.551
	(1.738)	(1.724)	(1.873)	(2.353)	(1.439)
No. of market trucks	.204	−.257	−.346	.861[a]	.141
	(.319)	(.304)	(.294)	(.387)	(.270)
Crop auction present	.182	−.108	−.488	.156	−.241
	(.246)	(.235)	(.268)	(.495)	(.229)
Intercept	8.777	5.458	−.635	4.169	4.560
Pearson goodness-of-fit X^2	40.927	42.537	37.811	35.190	45.020
	39df	39df	39df	39df	39df

Note: Standard errors of regression coefficients are in parentheses.
[a]$p < .05$.

affected assembler use of more than one channel of sale. Limitations on selecting more than one channel would provide additional evidence of restricted market access.

Probit Analysis

Probit analysis is a multivariate regression technique suitable when dependent variables are dichotomous and binary as they are in the present study (e.g., use or non-use of the rural auction channel). Analyzing the survey data with this technique allows us to assess further the effects of village-level conditions on village assemblers' use of different crop marketing channels (Table 1).

The most striking result of the analysis indicates that working capital is the only factor that broadly influences village assemblers' marketing choices.[7] First, working capital negatively predicts the assembler's use of a rural auction and positively predicts the sale of crops to the urban auction and urban merchant. Second, working capital negatively predicts selling to a rural agent at a significance level that approaches the .05 criterion.[8] In short, village assemblers with more working capital are more likely to sell in urban channels, where the returns are greater, and are less likely to sell in rural channels, where they are less. The reverse is true of village assemblers with less working capital.

The survey found huge disparities in the working capital available to village assemblers. For example, the smallest assembler in the sample spent only 50 L.S. to purchase crops in 1981–82, compared with 197,610 L.S. spent by the largest assembler. The median of 3409 L.S. points to a skewing of village assemblers toward the low end. In other words, most village assemblers operated with rather low amounts of working capital while a few had access to very high amounts.

The distribution of working capital among village assemblers is not a matter of chance but is associated with some characteristics of the villages. Marked variation in the distribution of working capital (Table 2) exists both between villages (comparing means) as well as within villages (comparing the size of the standard deviations with their means). It appears that in some of the villages a dual structure of village assemblers exists: there is a marked disparity between large and small crop assemblers as measured by working capital. (The standard deviations are as large or larger than their means.)

Two other factors are revealed to have a much more limited sphere of influence. The number of market trucks in the village encourages direct sales to urban merchants. Since sales directly to an urban merchant are likely to entail transporting untaxed or undertaxed crops and since the truck operator must be a party to this operation, it is reasonable to believe that having a truck in one's own village facilitates discussion and planning of these unlawful activities, not to mention the trust that is fostered through kinship and coresidential ties. The probit analysis also detects a tendency for the presence of a government-sponsored rural auction to preclude urban auction sales, again at a significance level that is nearly .05. The reason for this relationship is probably the fact that the necessary taxes have already been assessed at the rural auction.

These are the only noteworthy relationships revealed by the probit

Table 2
Breakdown of Village Assemblers' Working Capital
(in L.S.) by Village

Village	Population	Mean	Standard Deviation	Cases
Wardass	400	71,505	0	1
Ayara	800	38,536	42,999	4
Abu Haraz	5,000+	35,071	72,547	7
Kazgeil	5,000	13,223	8,672	5
el-Kharta	2,000	12,780	18,056	4
Umm Kuka	400	4,721	875	2
Umm Sot	700	4,356	5,054	2
el-Geifil	600	2,954	2,946	2
Umm Ramad	3,700	2,609	2,595	8
el-Hammadiya	1,200	2,245	1,143	5
Bagbage	200	2,175	1,746	2
Umm Sabagha	140	686	0	1
Burbur	500	180	183	2
Total	20,640+	14,443	33,874	45

Note: 1.000 L.S. = $0.90 US in December 1981

analysis, and they make sense in terms of the ethnographic observations made during the study.[9] Interestingly, none of the village-level conditions predicts assembler use of more than one channel versus only one channel for marketing crops. This leads me to conclude that village assemblers are not compelled to sell in only one channel by their level of working capital or any of the other factors considered.

The probit analysis gives further evidence that village-level conditions do not in general pose barriers to marketing channel use by village assemblers in the el-Obeid system. Perhaps the most important finding in this regard is that neither the number of trucks in the village nor the absence of a rural auction restricts the use of rural auctions by village assemblers. This fact is important because the rural auction allows small village assemblers to market crops at competitive prices and keep abreast of price movements in the urban auction at el-Obeid.

Working capital alone was shown to have a far-reaching impact on village assemblers' participation in the marketing system. But even though village assemblers with large amounts of capital can sell in higher-return channels more easily than small assemblers, small assemblers can still have choices to make. They are not compelled to sell in only one channel. On the whole, therefore, the el-Obeid marketing system seems reasonably flexible and efficient for this category of participants.

These findings do not automatically transfer to the situation of agricultural producers, of course. Market opportunities would not necessarily appear equally benign to producers even though, on the face of it, producers have a considerable range of choice (Figure 2). I have shown previously (Reeves 1989) that the size of the producer's production strongly influences whether crops are sold in one versus two or more channels and whether or not producers are likely to sell directly to a village assembler rather than sell in a higher-return channel. Greater flexibility and freedom of channel use is indicated for village assemblers than for producers, therefore, but this difference is probably not extreme.

CONCLUSION

The ethnographic and quantitative analyses above provide an important complement to the types of information that would have been gathered by a simple reliance on market margin and price analyses. For example, a market margin analysis during the period under study would probably have shown high margins for middlemen, particularly if the margins were compared to the interest rates of capital. These interest rates are typically subsidized by the government and are lower than the market rate which small producers and village entrepreneurs would have to pay. These results could lead to the conclusion that monopolistic power and other sources of inefficiency were prevalent in the el-Obeid marketing system. The policy recommendations stemming from this conclusion could lead to needless intervention through marketing boards or control of producer or consumer prices.

Price analysis would probably have shown that there was not a high correlation between the prices in different localities. This assumption might also lead to the conclusion that the government should intervene in marketing channels and control prices. In fact, this case study showed that village assemblers/shopkeepers provide a variety of economic services that are not monitored by these indirect measures and that any tendency toward exploitative pricing tends to be mitigated by (a) competition between village assemblers, (b) the fact that village assemblers and their clientele are often from the same extended families, and (c) the freedom of marketing choices which the system allows.

The anthropologist's interest in local settings can thus be a useful complement to more large-scale research strategies that have traditionally been used to assess market functioning. It is hoped that the methodology employed in this analysis will embolden anthropologists to engage in similar complementary policy research.

NOTES

This chapter has benefited significantly from comments by Tom Reardon and Jim Seale.

1. Economists—recognizing this shortcoming—have begun carrying out village-level studies of market behavior that would complement the indirect methods of assessing market efficiency and competitiveness. As a result, large-scale regional market surveys and individual research projects that focus on village markets showed a sharp increase since 1970 (e.g., Sherman, Shapiro, and Gilbert 1987; Eicher and Baker 1982; Norman, Simmons, and Hays 1982; Sherman 1981; Arizo-Nino et al. 1981; Herman 1979; Staatz 1979).

2. For a seminal collection of papers describing markets and traders in Sudan, see Manger (1984). Unfortunately, none of these papers deal with the el-Obeid Area.

3. The following year was disastrous for producers, but no data is available to show how the system responded to a severe test of this sort. Nor can we be certain how the system would respond to a banner year or to interannual fluctuations in the prices for sorghum, sesame, and groundnut. This lack of information points up the need in food policy analysis for longitudinal monitoring.

4. In December 1981, one Sudanese pound equaled $0.90 US.

5. In our survey, only two of the fifty-eight shopkeepers did not sell goods on credit, and both were located in a large village which had substantial numbers of teachers and government employees.

6. According to informants, there was no interest assessed in many cases. Shopkeepers explained that credit sales allowed them to move inventory dur-

ing the slow rainy season months and provided goodwill. Since goodwill was
an important factor in developing and maintaining a clientele, the foregone
interest charge amounted to a business promotion.

7. In this study, "working capital" was operationalized by surveying village
assemblers about their crop purchases during the 1981–82 marketing season.
They were asked about quantities of each crop purchased and prices paid.
Summing across food commodities for quantities purchased and multiplying
by the price provided an estimate of the "working capital" of each village
assembler. Of course, this approach would yield only an approximation. Since
this method required crop assemblers to recall events several months in the
past, it is possible that error has been introduced due to faulty memory. However, it was my strong impression that village assemblers and shopkeepers have
prodigious memories for their business activities, a fact that is strengthened
by the general lack of volatility in village prices during a season. Another
source of error could be that information was consciously withheld from me
and the other surveyors. I suspect this is particularly true of the sale of crops
to urban merchants since there is a strong possibility that these crops were sold
without taxes having been assessed. Nevertheless, and bearing these caveats
in mind, the data seem to represent acceptable order-of-magnitude estimates
of the distribution of working capital.

8. The villages of Ayara, Abu Haraz, and el-Kharta show the greatest disparities in this regard. The case of Abu Haraz is not surprising. Lying south-
west of el-Obeid, it is the largest rural center in the area of our study and
boasts a broad array of economic institutions. Likewise, el-Kharta is one of
the largest villages lying in the drier regions north of el-Obeid. Ayara, on the
other hand, is a relatively small village. However, Ayara is uniquely placed
on a major east-west transportation route and has an unusual diversity of economic services for its size because it is a truck stop. Furthermore, Ayara is the
major marketing center for a number of small villages in the area.

Kazgeil is another unusual case. It is nearly as large as Abu Haraz and has
a highly developed marketplace, but the distribution of working capital among
village assemblers is far more even than at Abu Haraz. In this case, the unique
factor is the presence of a Greek entrepreneur who has lived in the village for
several decades. At the time of the survey, the Greek was no longer involved in
crop assembling. His main enterprises were grain milling, cheesemaking, and
trucking. But many of the village assemblers in Kazgeil started out as partners
of this resourceful man. Over the years the Greek has sought to spur competition within the local market, and this competition accounts for the relatively
even distribution of working capital among the village assemblers at Kazgeil.

Two villages, Wardass and Umm Sabagha, are exceptional in another way.
Each has only one village assembler. Interestingly, these two villages stand

at virtually opposite ends of the scale of working capital. Umm Sabagha is a small, isolated hamlet of 140 inhabitants. The village assembler is also the village headman (the only occurrence of this dual role that we found) and is related to everyone in the village, which is made up of a single patrilineage. Quite a different circumstance exists at Wardass. This too is one of the smaller villages in the sample, having a population of around 400. But Wardass is a satellite of Abu Haraz and one of several villages recently settled in a locality where agricultural production was not extensive in the past so that soil fertility is high. As a consequence, the village assembler at Wardass does a booming business buying crops in his own and neighboring villages. The high level of working capital for the assembler at Wardass is somewhat misleading, however. Some of the money is not his own but is provided by a very large village assembler at Abu Haraz for whom he buys the crops on commission. Other examples of this kind of cooperative business venture between village assemblers were noted during the ethnographic investigations at Abu Haraz and Kazgeil.

The above discussion hints at some of the factors that are responsible for the disparities in the working capital available to village assemblers. Chief among these perhaps are village population size and the diversity of village economic institutions, but these factors in turn are influenced by water supply, soil composition and fertility, transportation routes, distance from el-Obeid, and unique circumstances such as the ones described above.

9. SPSS-X PROBIT routine provides correlation matrices for the independent variables in each model to determine multicollinearity. For all the analyses in Table 1, there were only weak to moderate correlations between the independent variables, demonstrating that multicollinearity is not a problem.

Inter- and Intrahousehold Income Allocation: Implications for Third World Food Policy

Roberta D. Baer

Food policy research has long recognized that household income is one of the key factors predicting dietary patterns. As income levels go up, it is assumed that households will increase their total purchases of food as well as their demand for more expensive, higher quality foods such as meats and dairy products. There is no question that income and relative prices are of prime importance in determining the food consumption patterns of a household (Berg 1973, Au Coin et al. 1972, Greiner and Latham 1981). However, just because income enters a household, or the hands of a member of a particular household, there is no guarantee that those funds will be used for food purchases. A primary issue is the amount of money available to those responsible for household expenditures (including food) and, secondly, how this amount of money is allocated among competing wants and needs. For example, there is no guarantee that food expenditures will win out over competing wants and needs for prestige consumer goods or higher priced but not as nutritionally beneficial foodstuffs. Therefore, the social and cultural factors which affect the patterns of who controls income and what they choose to do with it may be of equal or greater importance than aggregate income levels in understanding the effect of income increases on people's diets.

An alternative approach to modeling the relationship between income and dietary outcomes tries to itemize and understand the role of factors which determine *control over* income and how it is spent. This requires the introduction of a variable I will call "available income." Available income refers to the amount of money which is actually available to those in the household responsible for household expenditures, including food. The concept of available income is not related to who makes decisions on how the income is spent; it merely refers to the sum of money about which decisions on household expenditures are made by those in the household responsible for such decisions. Available income is not the same as "total food expenditure." Instead, it represents the total sum which is available to those who make decisions about *all* household expenditures, of which expenditures for food—which often have to compete with other wants and needs—are but one part. Factors which affect control over available income and how it is spent include:

- women's access to autonomous and semiautonomous sources of income,
- household structure and roles within the household,
- levels of home production of food,
- nutritional knowledge,
- competing desires for consumer goods, and
- ethnicity.

As a result of effects of these variables, households of similar total incomes may come to have differing amounts of available income and differing patterns of food consumption. This chapter examines the relationships of these variables to each other and to the process of income allocation through effects on available income. The utility of the concept in explaining income allocation patterns is then described for rural and urban households in northern Mexico.

DETERMINATION OF AVAILABLE INCOME

Three of the variables cited above are particularly important in determining the amount of available income: wives's access to autonomous and semiautonomous sources of income, economic roles and relations within the household, and the extent to which a household is involved in home production of food.

Much of the recent research on income allocation in relation to food consumption has focused on women's earnings. Women's incomes tend to be less seasonal than those of men, and in many parts of the world, women retain complete control over their earnings. In studies in West Africa (Dwyer 1983, Guyer 1980, Tripp 1982) and Kerala, India (Kumar 1978), increases in women's incomes have been associated with improvements in food consumption and/or nutritional status. The reason for this correlation seems to be that women, more than men, tend to spend their incomes on food or other household necessities, thus raising available income.

Some studies suggest that patterns of income allocation based on household role may be more important than those based on gender. For example, a wife's economic activity would have a greater impact on the amount of available income than that of a grown child, who may only give a portion or none of his/her earnings to the parents. Whitehead's work in northeastern Ghana illustrates the extent to which most members of a household retain control over their incomes. She found that "virtually all men, women, and children over 10 have some form of money income" (Whitehead 1981:94). Two-thirds of the households consist of between five and twenty adults, and "no other person has rights over an individual's cash income" (Whitehead 1981:100).

Data from Mexico City also reflected that there was no general pattern for the extent to which grown children contributed to household expenses (Beneria and Roldan 1987). The mother's ability to convince her children to contribute and the economic situation of the particular household seemed to be the key variables. Even in cases where children did contribute, they typically contributed at most only a portion of their earnings (Beneria and Roldan 1987).

The extent to which a household produces some of the food it consumes, decreasing out-of-pocket expenditures for food, also affects the amount of available income. Much of the problem of declines in nutritional status associated in some studies with the shift from subsistence to market production (Fleuret and Fleuret 1980) is actually a problem of declining available income. Households cannot afford to buy back the quality of diet they once home-produced. Even small amounts of home production (as from a family garden) can have significant positive impact on food consumption (Smith et al. 1983) because the available income of the household is increased.

ALLOCATION OF AVAILABLE INCOME

An increase in available income does not necessarily translate directly into a proportional increase in food expenditures or a proportional improvement in the quality or quantity of the household's diet. Instead, household food consumption is often dependent on the allocation of available income. For example, increased economic activity of women may increase the amounts of money over which they have control and/or their roles in household decisionmaking with regard to expenditures. The extent to which an increased control over income or decisionmaking translates into dietary changes may be related to nutritional knowledge of the wife as well as to relative desires for prestige foods and consumer goods.

Nutritional knowledge is an important variable in determining patterns of allocation of available income since even if low income is a constraint, efficient utilization of actual resources can produce a more adequate diet. Traditional diets were the result of centuries of cultural knowledge about what foods to consume and how to combine them. The transition to market from subsistence economies has supplied contemporary Third World societies with a wide range of new foods. Thus, the household has a variety of unfamiliar foods from which to select, without any cultural guidelines to suggest the most nutritional choices. The situation can be further worsened by the role of advertizing which seeks to promote the new foods, often convincing low-income households that consumption of high-priced products is necessary for good nutrition (Berg 1972).

Prestige values of particular foods may also cause changes in food consumption patterns, with use of low-prestige foods rejected (Devadas 1970, Cussler and de Give 1942). Low-prestige foods are usually those associated with the poor and include such items as sweet potatoes in the U.S. South (Fitzgerald 1976), bean curd in Hong Kong (Anderson and Anderson 1977), and wild greens in Mexico (Messer 1976). However, prestige foods may not be as nutritious as those which they replace (McKenzie 1974, Burgess and Dean 1962, Read 1964, den Hartog and Bornstein-Johansson 1976), though in most instances they are more expensive (Berg 1973).

Desires for consumer goods may also compete for available income. Again, cash income is often used to purchase consumer goods which confer prestige (Marchione 1980). Such items often include clothing, radios, and bicycles (den Hartog and Bornstein-Johansson 1976). The importance of certain types of consumer goods as symbols of prestige should not be underestimated. Simic (1973) reported that rural Yugoslavian villagers often bought radios and displayed them prominently as prestige items—despite the fact that their homes lacked the electricity necessary to make the radios work.

ETHNICITY

Ethnicity is an important variable which affects both the amount of available income and the way in which it is allocated. Ethnic patterns of income control and allocation and household residential patterns (for example, whether nonnuclear family working adults reside together and pool or separate income) affect the amount of available income. Residential patterns which allow other household members to help with cooking and childcare can mitigate the negative effects on household nutrition sometimes attributed to the lack of time working women have for household activities (Popkin and Solon 1976).

The allocation of family available income is greatly influenced by cultural patterns of decisionmaking. Especially important is the extent to which female participation is limited or encouraged.

Ethnic patterns of home food production may also play an important role in determining available income. Ethnic background will also affect traditional food choices and help determine the degree to which the family incorporates foods which the larger society deems of high prestige value into the household diet. For example, ethnic groups trying to assimilate into the larger society may strive to emulate mainstream eating habits. Thus, Eskimo diets presently include such items as soft drinks, crackers, and potato chips (Kemp 1971). Groups trying to maintain distinct identities may deliberately avoid the foods of the larger society and choose another outside reference group whose food habits they emulate. For example, the Hokkien Chinese in Malaysia, who seek to differentiate themselves from the Malaysians, avoid Malay foods, while using those foods which they associate with the higher prestige western societies (Anderson and Anderson 1977).

Figure 1
Sonora in the Context of the United States and Mexico

From *Urban Anthropology* 16, no. 1 (1987): 44. By permission of *Urban Anthropology*.

CASE STUDY METHODOLOGY

The ways the above variables affect available income and its allocation can be seen in data collected in Sonora, a state in northwestern Mexico (Figure 1), where ethnographic and dietary research were carried out in 1982.[1] Factors affecting income allocation patterns were studied in four groups: (1) residents (20 households) of the rural village of Arroyo Lindo,[2] (2) permanent migrants (20 households) from the Arroyo Lindo region to the state capital of Hermosillo, (3) urban-born people (38 households) who had been raised in Hermosillo, and

(4) U.S. citizens (27 households) who had settled permanently in Hermosillo. Each household had both male and female heads (i.e., husband and wife), both of whom were under sixty years old, and at least two children.

Referrals from informants who lived in different areas of the village were used to locate the twenty rural households in the Arroyo Lindo sample. These households satisfied the above criteria; in addition, either the husband or wife had a sibling who was married to an individual who had migrated from Arroyo Lindo to Hermosillo. The migrant sample consisted of the urban relatives of the Arroyo Lindo household sample; the rural households provided the addresses. Selection of the urban-born sample was more difficult. Since most urban residents in Hermosillo were migrants, it was harder to find households in which both heads had been born in the city. A system of using networks very similar to the strategy used in Arroyo Lindo was therefore used to select the urban-born households. People who had been born in Hermosillo were asked to suggest families who met the sample criteria. A number of different networks in different areas of the city and from different income strata were employed. The community of U.S. citizens (referred to below as "Americans") was defined as all households in which the wife was a U.S. citizen and who were living permanently in Mexico. This community was quite small, and all of the households which met the sample criteria were included in the study. The backgrounds of the women were both Anglo-American (i.e., citizens of non-Mexican ancestry) and Mexican-American, but in all cases the women considered their nationality to be American.

Each group was representative of a wide range of incomes; however, for some of the analyses presented, the groups were divided into low (less than or equal to 49,000 pesos, $1,225 US) and high (greater than 49,000 pesos) income groupings of per capita annual income. The value of the peso at the time of the study was equal to $.025 US. Due to differing sizes of the sample groups, when analyses of the data cross-cut these groups, the data were weighted.

Income data were collected through ethnographic interviewing on various aspects of the topic of income allocation, including how much each worker contributed to either the husband or wife, how the income of each household member was used, how decisions were made on household expenditures, and how increased income would be spent.

Total income refers to the total amount of income earned by all workers in the household. Available income is a calculated variable and refers to the total amount of money that reached the husband and/or wife, i.e., the total of each of their earnings plus whatever contributions they received from other working members of their households. All income data given represent mean per capita annual income levels. Three-day dietary data were collected on each of the households.

Data on the twenty-seven American households is only presented in the ethnicity section below. The discussion of other variables refers only to the seventy-eight rural, migrant, and urban-born households.

RESULTS

Household Structures and Roles Within the Household

Focusing on the first three subsample groups (rural, migrant, and urban-born), the research in Sonora supports the literature cited above on the distinction between role and gender in terms of effects on income allocation, amount of available income, and effects on food consumption patterns. Role (household head vs. child or other relative) proves to be the more important variable. Cultural norms call for all adults, even grown but unmarried children, to live with either their family of orientation or other members of their extended families. As such, households often consisted of many workers, and the income of each person was his or hers to dispose of as he or she saw fit. Husbands and wives were responsible for the allocation of available income and tended to use most of their own earnings for household expenses. Only a portion of the income earned by other household members was contributed to the household heads to be used for household expenses.

The seventy-eight rural, migrant, and urban-born households could be further subdivided into two types—those in which only head(s) of household were employed (hereafter referred to as Head(s) Works or HW households), numbering forty-six, and those in which additional members of the household were employed (MW or Multiple Worker Households), numbering 32. While no significant differences are seen in per capita total household income levels[3] of the two types of households (mean 3.4 in both cases), per capita available income level drops significantly (p ≤ .01, one tailed) in the MW households (from a mean of 3.4 to a mean of 2.8). Thus the male and/or female head(s) of households with multiple workers who were in charge of making key expenditures, including food, had less mean per capita income with which to make these allocation decisions than did households in which only the head(s) of household were employed.

Household Structure vs. the Importance of Wife's Income

Based on the literature, dietary improvements in households in which the wife has a source of income were anticipated. However, in this study, the presence of a working wife did not result in positive dietary effects—increased quantity and quality of the diet—for three of the sample groups (rural, migrant, and urban-born).

Yet, when analyses were conducted which controlled for household structure (MW vs. HW), positive types of dietary effects of a working wife were observed—but only in the HW households. This pattern is probably because of the fact that 63 percent of the working wives lived in MW households, with noted disparities between total and available income levels. Although the wife is contributing to the available income, this income, along with that of the husband, is divided among a greater number of additional consumers. These other employed consumers were not contributing to the same extent to the household's expenditures.

The presence of a working wife did not necessarily result in improved diets among the MW households in general. It did, however, make a significant difference for MW as well as HW households at the lower income levels. In MW households of lower available income levels, the presence of an economically active wife results in increased consumption of fruit, eggs, and meat, and decreased use of dairy products and potatoes. In HW households of similar low-available-income levels, the presence of an economically active wife is associated with an increase in fruit, vegetable, dairy, and miscellaneous foods (high-calorie, low-nutrient foods such as chips, soda, candy, etc.) and a decrease in use of beans, eggs, and grains. Thus, the pattern of food consumption for households of lower available income involves a substitution of foods with higher nutrient densities—with particular improvement suggested in vitamin intakes.

These effects of wives' economic activity for the lower income

Woman shelling corn, rural Sonora, Mexico. Photograph by R. Baer.

groups were evident in spite of the fact that only 45 percent of the wives reported spending their incomes on food as opposed to other household needs such as children's clothing. The most important issue seemed to be that wives with their own sources of income were better able to deal with unexpected expenses than were wives who did not have access to such funds. Such unexpected expenses included children's schoolbooks, medicine, or unexpectedly high utility bills. Wives without their own incomes were generally forced to meet these expenses by asking their husbands for money in excess of their usual allotment for household needs (thus indicating that they were failing in their roles as capable household managers) or by reducing spending on food to make the usual allotment stretch to meet the unexpected needs. Wives with their own sources of income were generally in a better position to cover unexpected expenses without having to raid the family food budget because they could just make up the shortfall themselves.

Cultural and Prestige Factors Affecting Wives' Access to Income

While the economic activity of wives was evident in all three of the Mexican subsample groups (rural, migrant, urban-born), it was highest in rural and migrant households, regardless of income level, and in higher-income urban-born women (Baer, in press). This fact may be related to the low prestige of women's work. Among the lower-income urban-born, working women tend to be single, divorced, abandoned, or those who are unwed mothers, often employed in occupations of very low prestige, such as in positions as maids. Thus, urban-born women may feel that choosing to be economically active implies that either they have no man to support them or that their husband is unable or unwilling to do so. In urban higher-income groups, women's work tends to be invisible—often taking place in the home. If visible, working women in this group tend to work in occupations of high prestige, such as in the professions. In contrast, the migrant wives continue the rural patterns of high rates of economic activity, even working in low-prestige types of work. They are either unaware of urban norms, or their desire to get ahead causes them to ignore such values.

Household Production and Consumption of Food and Consumer Goods

Household production of food was seen to be an important factor in all three of the Mexican populations studied, even in the urban areas. Different patterns of planting fruit trees and keeping chickens—which raised available income—were evident among migrant and urban-born populations, with the migrants more involved in such activities. These differences in home food production were reflected in the respective qualities of the diets of the two groups. Particularly at lower income levels, migrant diets were better than those of the urban-born.

The selective retention by the migrants of a number of nutritionally as well as economically advantageous rural food consumption patterns produce higher quality diets and raise available income. These practices included use of the rural dish of a *caldo* (thick soup) at midday as opposed to the urban pattern of a *sopa* (a pasta or rice dish, such as Spanish rice). While *caldos* are of higher nutritional value, they are of much lower prestige than are *sopas*. Migrants also tend to use more homemade tortillas, while the urban-born prefer the higher-prestige but higher-priced store-bought bread.

Desires for consumer goods are strong in this area of Mexico, and data indicate that trade-offs are sometimes made between diet and consumer goods purchases. Households that had just purchased either a television or vehicle exhibited a decrease in consumption of fruit, vegetables, dairy products, eggs, and meat while use of beans, grains, and potatoes increased (Baer 1988).

The Sonora study did not reveal that wives' nutritional knowledge significantly affected food consumption patterns. Greater nutritional knowledge tended to be associated with higher-income levels. The extent to which programs designed to increase nutritional knowledge would affect food consumption patterns is not clear, especially given the limited available incomes of those with less nutritional knowledge.

Ethnicity

The study showed significant differences between the two ethnic groups (Mexican and American) in terms of the dietary effects of women's work. As there were no American households of lower-income levels living in Hermosillo, these conclusions about the role of ethnicity were attained only by comparing the upper-income Americans of Hermosillo with their urban-born Mexican neighbors of similar income levels. Economic activity of Mexican wives was associated with decreased consumption of some types of foods, such as fruit, miscellaneous foods (high-calorie, low-nutrient foods such as chips, soda, and candy), and meat, and increased use of dairy products. No significant differences in dietary patterns were found among American households with economically active and non-economically active wives. This pattern may be because of the greater dependence of the American women in the study on time-saving canned foods and mixes; the Mexicans have a cultural preference for use of fresh food and cooking from scratch, both of which are much more time-consuming.

IMPLICATIONS FOR FOOD POLICY

The Mexico case study illustrates the way social and cultural factors influence the manner in which income is or is not translated into dietary improvements. In particular, the case study highlights the important role of economic roles and relations within the household as key factors affecting the extent to which income increases are likely to be translated into higher available income. Households in which there are multiple workers in addition to the male and/or female household head(s) tend to be those with the lowest per capita available incomes. Similar factors may be active in other parts of the developing world and may be at least partly responsible for the frequently observed noncorrelations between income and nutritional status (Berg 1973). More specifically, these data suggest that these noncorrelations might disappear if per capita *available income* (i.e., the income actually under the control of the individuals who purchase household food supplies) were used in analyses instead of total household income.

Furthermore, a differentiation needs to be made between wives' work and women's work, in terms of its effects on household diet. Women other than the wife often have sources of income, but they behave as do the males who are not the husband, i.e., only a portion, at best, of their income becomes "available." Although the economic activities of wives in the Mexican case study were important to the household income, they were not sufficient in the households in which there were multiple workers in addition to the household head(s) to overcome the effects of increasing consumption (without income pooling). But particularly at the lower income levels, which are those most likely to be at nutritional risk, whether or not the wife had a separate income became an important factor in both types (HW and MW) of households. The nutritional risk of lower-income, multiple-worker households would be predicted to increase greatly in the absence of the earnings of those wives.

A critical preliminary issue, then, in the development of effective food policies becomes the determination of the household level behaviors and situations which cause the same amounts of total household income to result in different amounts of available income. This analysis must then be supplemented by investigation into the social, cultural, and economic factors which influence how available income will be spent.

While the "problem" of lack of correspondence between total household income and available income can be avoided by focusing on household expenditures as opposed to income, such an approach is less helpful in determining policy directions in that it accepts the reductions in total household income made by allocation patterns and decisions without explaining all the important processes and factors which drive those decisions. Determination for a particular cultural group of the general ways in which household decisions determine amount and allocation of available income reveals the critical variables in each situation, and appropriate policies to affect those variables then can be formulated.

Food and agricultural policies must be evaluated in terms of the effects they will have on the available incomes of the households involved. Planners should seek to focus on programs with the greatest potential for increasing available incomes. Furthermore, if a project cannot avoid manipulation of a variable, such as wives' work, which would be expected to decrease available income or change the ways in which available income is allocated, other programs should be developed as part of the project which could compensate for this by manipulation of another factor, such as home production of food, which would increase available income. Policy planners who have a more indepth understanding of the factors which determine available income and how it is allocated are in a better position to develop these sorts of counterbalancing programs.

In summary, the essence of effective food policy is the manipulation of key variables to improve dietary patterns and nutritional status. It has long been recognized that increasing people's income is an important way to begin this process. The key contribution of the concept of "available income" is to highlight some of the cultural and social factors which affect control of household income as well as the allocation of household income for food and other needs. By clarifying these relationships *prior* to the design of food policies, planners can develop more effective programs.

NOTES

1. This research was funded by the International Food Policy Research Institute. Additional support was provided by the Comins Fund (University of Arizona) and the Centro de Investigacion en Alimentacion y Desarrollo (Hermosillo, Mexico).

2. A pseudonym has been used to protect anonymity of informants.

3. Household income levels are as follows:

level 1: 0–12,000 pesos
level 2: 12,001–32,000 pesos
level 3: 32,001–49,000 pesos
level 4: 49,001–68,000 pesos
level 5: 68,001 + pesos

Integrating Nutritional Concerns into Adaptive Small Farm Research Programs

Kathleen M. DeWalt

Several decades after the beginning of the Green Revolution, a conservative estimate of 500 million people continue to experience hunger or malnutrition (Poleman 1981). Although the victims of periodic famine capture our attention most dramatically, subtler, chronic malnutrition is probably far more important in limiting the survival of children and the capabilities of adults. The greatest proportion of the hungry is found in rural, agricultural communities of the Third World—the beneficiaries of several decades of Green Revolution technology in agricultural production.

Dramatic increases in the potential and real productivity of food crops have often not had positive impacts on the food consumption and nutrition of rural people for a number of reasons. First, although many research efforts and many agricultural projects explicitly include the goal of improving food consumption and nutritional status, they rarely attempt to address this goal directly. Second, projects often fail to reach those at greatest nutritional risk, in part because project activities and technologies frequently benefit those farmers who have greater resources at the initiation of a project. This was true of the introduction of Green Revolution technology, at least in its earlier stages (Lipton and Longhurst 1985). Third, programs and projects often fail to appreciate the complex nature of the relationships between agricultural production, income, and food consumption and nutritional status. These relationships are social, cultural, and economic, as well as biological and ecological. Few strategies for agricultural development anticipate the effects of technological change on patterns of consumption, specifically food consumption, and ultimately nutritional status.

Finally, as Pinstrup-Anderson (1981) has pointed out, there are a number of competing goals for agricultural policy, research, and technology transfer. The priorities assigned to competing goals—such as stimulating export earnings, promoting growth of Gross National Product (GNP), maintaining cheap food policies, and even promoting national self-sufficiency in foodstuffs—may compete with the improvement of food consumption for the rural population.

For agricultural research and development to have a positive impact on the food consumption and nutrition of the rural poor, policymakers must make improving nutritional status an explicit goal from the start of program planning and implementation. Once policymakers have identified improved nutritional status as an explicit policy goal (rather than as a by-product of attaining other goals), they must develop strategies to address food consumption issues directly for groups with identified resource constraints and opportunities, within the policy environment of specific countries and regions.

In this chapter I review the literature which discusses the desirability and feasibility of explicitly including food consumption and nutrition goals in agricultural research and development projects. Based on this review, I conclude that what is needed is a framework to give policymakers guidelines for the analysis of food consumption and nutrition information and the incorporation of this information into the design, implementation, and evaluation of agricultural projects. I then present a framework for identifying nutrition constraints and opportunities in particular projects and analyzing the potential effects of projects on the food consumption and nutrition of limited resource farmers. Four research steps are discussed which enhance the chances that food consumption goals will be incorporated into the actual design and monitoring of agricultural research programs.

Illustrations in this chapter are drawn from the general literature as well as my own experience with agricultural research projects in Honduras, Mexico, and Ecuador.[1]

BACKGROUND: WHY INCLUDE NUTRITIONAL AND CONSUMPTION GOALS IN AGRICULTURAL RESEARCH AND DEVELOPMENT?

The relationships between agricultural production, food consumption, and subsequent nutritional status have received a great deal of attention in recent years. This increased attention has been primarily a result of disenchantment with other approaches to improving nutritional status, such as nutrition education and supplementary feeding programs; a recognition of the failure of reliance on economic growth to "trickle down" or to materially improve the status of the rural poor; and a recognition of the potential impact of agricultural change on food consumption.

Limitations of Nutrition Interventions and Economic Growth Strategies

Although the "new nutrition education" currently being advocated may have an impact on mothers' knowledge and practices with respect to the feeding of small children, we have argued for a number of years that issues of food availability and access to resources have a greater impact on food consumption than nutrition knowledge for the rural poor (DeWalt and Pelto 1977; DeWalt 1983a). Similarly, a review of supplemental feeding programs for small children (Beaton and Ghessimi 1979) revealed that small, carefully monitored pilot projects can be successful but that large-scale implementation of supplemental feeding programs have little or no impact on the community's nutritional status. In fact, the nutritional status of some program participants was even found to have deteriorated in comparison with nonparticipants (Kennedy and Pinstrup-Andersen 1984). At best, supplemental feeding and other nutritional interventions appear to be best suited for improvement of specific nutritional problems in small target groups at special risk (Pinstrup-Andersen 1981).

Reliance on general economic growth to have a trickle-down effect on the quality of life of the nutritionally at-risk has come to be seen as naive given the current understanding of the relationships between general economic growth and increases in inequality. Increasing growth (GNP) has usually been associated with increases in the marginalization of poorer citizens (Molina 1983). In market-oriented developing countries, economic growth is unlikely to reduce significantly the prevalence of malnutrition (Selowsky 1979; Knudson and Scandizzo 1979; Pinstrup-Andersen and Caicedo 1978; Pinstrup-Andersen 1981). Even programs aimed at improving the income of rural families at nutritional risk may not have a positive impact on nutritional status for a variety of reasons (DeWalt 1983a, 1983b; Bouis et al. 1985).

Effects of Agricultural Change on Food Consumption

Anthropologists have long recognized that the introduction of new technology almost always brings about a reorganization of production activities. This reorganization in turn sets in motion a series of other changes in distribution and consumption, especially food consumption.

One of the best examples of this is Nietschmann's (1973) now classic study of the effect of the commercialization of turtling on the Miskito Coast. As turtle hunting became a cash-earning enterprise, it led to the reallocation of labor and other resources from gardening to turtling, the breakdown of a traditional method of distribution of turtle meat, and the subsequent partial replacement of turtle meat with purchased starches in the Miskito diet.

Two studies assessing the impact of Plan Chontalpa in Tabasco, Mexico (Hernandez et al. 1974; Dewey 1980, 1981a, 1981b) show similar results. These evaluations showed that productivity increased dramatically as a result of the project but that only the nutritional status of the urban populations was improved. In particular, there was no real improvement in the nutritional status of the children of farm families although dietary patterns had changed as a result of a shift in consumption away from home production to the purchase of staple foods. Both studies showed a loss of dietary diversity with heavier reliance on a few staples.

Okere's (1983) monograph on diet among the Igbo notes a shift in production and consumption from more favored yams to less nutritious cassava in response to a loss of soil fertility. Soil fertility had declined due to an intensification of cultivation—the result of increasing population and competition from cash crops for both land and labor.

Lunven (1982) has reviewed six case studies in which United Nations Food and Agriculture Organization (FAO) development efforts failed to improve nutritional status or, in fact, contributed to nutritional decline among some segments of the population. He concludes that the projects failed to take into consideration patterns of land tenure, relationships among social and economic groups, patterning of labor demands, and scarcities of family labor at certain times. Also important were the local price effects of declines in food production that accompanied the promotion of cash crops. For most of the projects, those relatively better off were able to improve consumption while the groups at greatest nutritional risk were either untouched or had poorer access to food because of increases in the price of staple foods, loss of land, or loss of access to credit.

Postmortems such as these have lead to an increasing realization that agricultural technology is not nutritionally neutral and that the ways in which changing agricultural technology and agricultural development projects affect food consumption and nutritional status are not clearly understood or adequately examined.

Perhaps the most controversial area in which we can see a direct link between agricultural development and consumption is in development strategies to promote commercial farming, which usually involves re- placing subsistence crops with cash crops. The underlying assumption of these interventions is usually that increases in income will enable the producer to purchase displaced foods. As our earlier work in Mexico suggests, however, increasing income may provide a *different* diet but not necessarily a *better* diet (DeWalt 1983b). Several recent reviews on the income and nutrition impacts of increased emphasis on cash crops note a number of subsequent economic and social shifts that can have a detrimental effect on nutritional status (Bouis et al. 1985; Braun and Kennedy 1986; Maxwell and Fernando 1988; Maxwell 1988). Among the areas of concern related to this commercialization of agriculture are (1) potential improvements in cash income without improvement in total income; (2) differences in the amount of income allocated to food as a function of the sources and control of income (is it generated and controlled by men or women?) or of the lumpiness of income (the ex- tent to which income arrives in lump sums to the family); (3) shifts in work patterns and labor demands (especially of women); (4) changes in family structure as a result of changes in labor demand and seasonal or permanent migration; (5) shifts in the allocation of resources within the household, including food; (6) local and regional increases in food prices resulting in a loss of real income; (7) changes in land tenure; and (8) increasing dependency as a result of monopolistic control of inputs and monopsony.

Several recent studies of increasing cash production in Africa, where land availability is not the most important constraint, show that real increases in income, as a result of promotion of cash cropping, do trans- late into increases in food consumption and nutritional status (Kennedy and Cogill 1988; Braun 1988). The question remains, however, as to what the effects may be in situations in which land is a major constraint. As Maxwell (1988), Braun and Kennedy (1986), Longhurst (1988), DeWalt et al. (1988), and others have noted, the potential for positive or negative effects of shifts from semisubsistence to cash cropping is strongly dependent on the social, economic, policy, and physical environments; the nature of the existing farming system; and the crops being introduced. Therefore, existing research is contradictory and difficult to compare (Braun and Kennedy 1986). In addition it also suggests the need to empirically assess social, economic, environmental, and policy contexts, as well as to understand existing farming systems during project development and implementation.

The application of new technologies to subsistence cropping systems is another well-documented area where changes in production can have a direct impact on consumption. Monocropping, for example, may result in a decline in crop diversity, which in turn decreases dietary diversity. New cropping practices may also result in the elimination of unplanted food-producing crops such as edible wild plants that grow in the disturbed soils between rows of cultivated crops. While these displaced minor crops and uncultivated plants may provide a major source of micronutrients, their value is often overlooked because such plants do not provide the bulk of energy in food consumption (Messer 1972, 1977; DeWalt 1983a).

Technologies requiring reallocation of labor among family members may also have dramatic effects on the nutritional status of family members. Some have argued that the commercialization of agriculture results in a diversion of food resources from nonproductive members of the household (i.e., children) to working members of the household (Gross and Underwood 1971; Fleuret and Fleuret 1980; Bouis et al. 1985). Workers may also need to satisfy increased energy requirements resulting from changes in production practices.

The introduction of new technology which is appropriate for men but not for women may divert resources away from women's production activities (Braun 1988). In the Gambia, for example, the introduction of new technology for the commercial cultivation of rice shifted control of rice production from women to men.

Some technologies and crops demand more labor, increasing the already heavy labor demands on women and, sometimes, children. Moreover, changes in agricultural technology can affect the prevalence of infections that, in turn, add to nutritional stress. For example, the effect of irrigation on schistosomiasis rates in some countries is well known, while the effect on malaria rates of the emergence of pesticide resistant mosquitos—the result of indiscriminate use of agricultural insecticides—is just beginning to be appreciated.

To summarize, changes in production such as increased commercialization and the adoption of new technology have a host of social, structural, and economic effects which in turn affect diet and nutrition. An approach to understanding the effects of production changes at the community level must encompass the effects on control of resources, social stratification (locally and at higher levels), family organization, migration, wage laborers, tenant farmers and sharecroppers (i.e., on land tenure), and on different types of nonfarm income-generating activities.

Effects of Food Consumption on Agricultural Change

Just as agricultural change affects consumption, the consumption goals of small farmers can affect agricultural change. Small farmers producing crops for consumption within the household as well as for sale understand the need to protect family diets. They evaluate new varieties of seed and production techniques on the basis of their impact on the acceptability of the product as food, as well as on their productivity and agronomic properties. Numerous accounts exist of the rejection of seeds because their food quality characteristics were unacceptable. In Honduras, for example, we found that farmers' perceptions of unacceptable food characteristics of new varieties of sorghum accounted for the fact that they were adopted only as cash crops.

Consumption goals are affected by food processing characteristics as well as taste. In many cases food processing techniques (for example, how long a variety has to cook, how long it takes to grind) were ignored.

THE FRAMEWORK: INCLUDING FOOD CONSUMPTION AND NUTRITION CONCERNS IN AGRICULTURE RESEARCH AND DEVELOPMENT

The notion that agricultural research, technology development, and specific development projects should have improved nutritional status as a direct goal is certainly not new. A review of the efforts of the International Agricultural Research Centers (IARCs) (Pinstrup-Andersen, Berg, and Forman 1984) demonstrates that most of the IARCs include improvement of nutrition as a goal of their research, although few IARCs now have programs that specifically address questions of human nutrition. Our reviews of project papers for the United States Agency for International Development (USAID) show that improved nutrition for the farm family is a goal in the majority of small farm focused research and development projects. However, neither the IARCs nor the greater part of USAID projects explicitly include strategies for addressing nutrition concerns in project planning or implementation, nor do they include food consumption or nutritional parameters in evaluation. Based on the reviews, our conclusion was that there was a strong need for a framework for the analysis of food consumption and nutrition information to allow for more explicit consideration of this information at different stages of the project cycle.

Over the last decade and a half, the need to understand the logic behind existing patterns of production, especially among resource-poor farmers—an important aspect of farming systems research (*see* Hansen, this volume)—has come to be accepted as a first step toward the introduction of change in these systems. With the increased realization that changes in production may be linked to changes in consumption, as noted above, we have come to advocate the inclusion of an analysis of patterns of consumption and the factors affecting them, or, in other words, an analysis of the nutrition system (DeWalt, 1981, 1983a; DeWalt and DeWalt 1987) in addition to an analysis of the farming system in project planning and design. As an aid to organizing the interrelationships between the farming system and the nutrition system, we focus on a series of linkages between production and consumption. One or several of these key linkages may be addressed in project design and implementation of case study projects. Frankenberger (1985) has summarized much of the literature on linkages between agricultural production and food consumption, and this synopsis draws heavily on his work. Other key works include Pinstrup-Andersen (1981), Pines (1983), Longhurst (1983), and Swaminathan (1984).

The linkages outlined below offer foci for agricultural research and development efforts by outlining specific areas of the nutrition system and its interrelationship with the farming system that should be analyzed. At the same time they represent areas that must be taken into consideration for projects to avoid negative impacts on food consumption and nutritional status.

Food Preference, Acceptability, and Utilization

There are countless tales of the failure of improved varieties of food crops to be adopted by farmers or to have an impact on the diets of small-farm families because the improved variety did not have acceptable food quality characteristics (Tripp 1984). For example, new varieties may produce foods unacceptable to local tastes because of flavor or texture. In other instances the cooking qualities of varieties require changes in food preparation techniques. They may, for example, require a longer cooking time and hence more fuel and more of the meal-maker's time. Food crops that do not meet local preferences are unlikely to be adopted or are likely to be produced as a commercial crop rather than a subsistence crop. For example, while sorghum is a food grain in southern Honduras, some introduced hybrid sorghums are grown only as a cash crop because they do not produce acceptable tortillas (DeWalt and DeWalt 1982).

Potential food crops introduced to areas in which they have not been traditionally used as food are unlikely to be used as subsistence crops without an acceptable utilization package—a set of preparation techniques that meets local needs. The International Institute of Tropical Agriculture (IITA) examined the effects of introducing an acceptable utilization package with their promotion of soybean production in communities in which there was no tradition of soybean consumption. The results indicated an increase in the number of farmers interested in producing soybeans and an increase in the proportion of production that was consumed within the household and community (IITA 1986).

A rapid reconnaissance survey of potato production and consumption in several areas of highland Ecuador (DeWalt, Uquillas, and Crissman 1989) showed that potatoes are prepared differently in different regions and a number of different potato dishes exist within each region. Production for home consumption involves several potato varieties in each region to provide potatoes with different characteristics suitable for the various dishes. Furthermore, the preferred varieties differ for each region. At the same time, potatoes for sale must meet the strong consumption preferences of the eventual consumers—often very different from the preferences of the producers. Therefore, recommendations for the organoleptic characteristics of improved varieties will be different for different regions and heterogeneous within regions.

Seasonality of Production, Crop Mix, and Minor Crops

Because of the seasonal dimension of agricultural production, small farmers in many areas of the world experience cyclical shortages of food as well as sharp peaks in human energy expenditure. In many instances the time of peak labor demand coincides with the most critical period for food availability. As a result, local tradition in a number of regions marks an identifiable "hungry season."

Agricultural research and development projects may address problems of seasonal hunger through the introduction of crops that mature during times of shortage, improved storage of crops, or the easing of labor demands during periods of food shortage. At the same time, crops and cultural practices that demand more labor during times of shortfall or exacerbate the seasonality of production should be avoided. In the same reconnaissance survey in three potato producing zones of Ecuador mentioned above, it was found that climatic conditions limit the production of potatoes to certain seasons in only some of the areas. In these areas, local potato varieties often are valued for their keeping qualities. In the areas in which year-round production is possible, storage properties are less important than taste preferences or agronomic properties (Uquillas et al. 1988). Consequently, recommendations to potato breeders stressed the importance of storage characteristics of potatoes for some regions and not for others.

Agricultural research and development should also address issues dealing with crop mix, such as the effect of shifts from subsistence or semisubsistence agriculture to more commercial agriculture. While the nutritional impact of agricultural commercialization is under considerable debate, introduction of commercial crops clearly can have a series of dietary impacts. While commercial crop production may increase income, it may also lead to a decline in crop diversity and dietary diversity, an exacerbation of the seasonality of production, increase in agricultural risk, decrease in real income, increase in local food prices, shifts in household division of labor and control over income, disruption of traditional means of food distribution and sharing, and increased pressure on land (Nietschmann 1973; Dewey 1980, 1981a, 1981b; Fleuret and Fleuret 1980; Pines 1983; Longhurst 1983; Bouis et al. 1985; Braun and Kennedy 1986).

In addition to the significant shifts that result from the commercialization of agriculture, the application of some agricultural technology and cultural practices to subsistence agriculture may have a negative effect on the availability of food. The use of monocropping techniques and herbicides may eliminate or reduce the cultivation of minor crops frequently intercropped with staples (Messer 1972, 1977). Wild food plants often grow as weeds in the disturbed soils in cultivated fields. In Central Mexico these "weeds" are called *carne de la milpa* (meat from the field) and constitute a crucial hungry season food (DeWalt 1983a). While minor crops and wild foods do not provide the bulk of energy and protein that staple grain and tuber crops supply, they may be the major sources of micronutrients in local diets.

On the other hand, programs that improve crop diversity and the production of minor crops—such as compound (backyard) gardening—can address the availability of micronutrients and have a beneficial effect on household diets.

Income

Many agricultural research and development projects expect to improve food consumption and nutritional status indirectly through improving the income of farm households. However, the relationships between agricultural income and food consumption are not straightforward.

First, the effect of changes in agricultural production on income depends on careful evaluation of production functions. Improvements in yield as a result of new agricultural technology or improved cultural practices may not result in improved net income if the cost, in cash or labor, is greater than the value of the output. We must extend this consideration to include social costs as well.

The commercialization of agriculture often means that while cash income may rise, real income may stagnate or may even decline. This is especially true if the cost of purchased food is greater than the imputed value of food previously produced for home consumption or if regional declines in food production occasion a rise in the price of food (Bouis et al. 1985).

Second, the effect of increased income on food consumption is a function of the form of income, the "lumpiness" of income and the source of income. Income in kind (i.e., in the form of food) is more likely to have a positive impact on food consumption than its equivalent in cash. The regularity in the flow of income tends to be more important than the amount of income (Pines 1983, USAID 1984a). Lumpy income is more likely to be spent on nonfood items. Finally, men and women have a tendency to spend income differently in many regions (*see* Baer, this volume). Income earned and controlled by women may be more likely to contribute to household food availability than income earned and controlled by men. By extension then, programs that even the flow of income, produce income in kind (improve food production), and differentially improve women's income are most likely to have a positive effect on food consumption.

The Role of Women in Production

"In rural economies, women are the pivot between production and consumption" (Longhurst 1983:44). In many parts of the world, especially in Africa, women are responsible for the greater part of food production. In areas of high cash cropping they may be entirely responsible. As noted above, women's income is more likely to be spent on food. In addition, women also frequently provide labor for the cultivation of their husband's cash crops or hire out their labor to others. In Africa and Latin America, women are actively involved in the commercialization of agricultural products. At the same time, women universally have the greatest responsibility for food preparation and childcare tasks that may compete with food production and income generation for women's time. Technology that increases demands on women's time or energy is likely to diminish the amount of time available for other crucial tasks, or the technology may fail to be adopted because the labor demands cannot be met.

Women are frequently ignored by agricultural extension services, although recommended changes in agricultural techniques may demand more household labor, including women's labor. The staff of the Adaptive Crops Research and Extension (ACRE) Project in Sierra Leone acknowledged that women provide the bulk of the labor and are in primary control of the food crops for which they were attempting to transfer technology, but none of the extension agents involved was a woman and all but three or four of the several hundred "contact farmers" were men. The staff certainly knew that their technology was not being adopted and would agree that the primary reason was that all of their recommendations increased the need for women's labor, already in short supply. The only successful innovation was a new sweet potato variety that matured several weeks earlier than traditional varieties and provided food during the hungry season (DeWalt 1987).

Special crop extension or home economics programs may not be the answer. Indeed, they may place even greater demands on women's time unless they include the extension of labor-saving techniques and devices.

Crop Labor Requirements

In addition to the food consumption effects associated with increases in labor demands of women, other effects associated with new crop labor requirements may also be important. Increases in labor demand and energy expenditure may not be offset by increases in income or food production. One result may be shifts in the intrahousehold distribution of resources and a diversion of food from less productive members of the household (children) to more economically crucial members (Fleuret and Fleuret 1980; Gross and Underwood 1971; Bouis et al. 1985). Even more likely is that new technology or cultural practices that demand significantly more labor will not be adopted and incorporated into small-farm agriculture even if there is an appreciable increase in production as noted in the ACRE Project.

Market Prices and Seasonality and Postharvest Storage

The importance of prices and markets is an issue that is often overlooked in agricultural research and development projects. Agricultural scientists have a tendency to overestimate the potential market for crops and the stability of prices. A market for a crop must exist, and the price effects of increased or decreased production must be taken into

Market vender, Tulcan, Ecuador. Photograph by K. DeWalt.

account. Dramatically increased production is likely to result in a reduction in prices, differentially penalizing the small producer. In addition, a decrease in price to the consumer may be accompanied by a displacement of labor and or a reduction in real wages. Lipton and Longhurst (1985) estimate that effects of the increases in yield as a result of the Green Revolution were offset by reductions in the price of crops and the wages of laborers/consumers. Finally, a decrease in the regional availability of foodstuffs accompanying a shift from food production to commercial cropping may raise local food prices and offset gains in income. In addition, small farmers frequently suffer from unfavorable terms of trade with respect to national as well as international markets (Latham 1984).

Although they are not directly an issue of agricultural production, problems in postharvest storage frequently affect food availability both directly by limiting the availability of home-produced food and indirectly by contributing to loss of income or lumpiness of income (when farmers need to sell the bulk of their crops immediately after harvest to minimize storage loss). In addition, postharvest storage problems are often addressed in research and extension packages. Research and extension efforts to improve storage, either through varietal development or work on storage pests and methods, are likely to have an important impact on food consumption.

STEPS TO INCORPORATE FOOD CONSUMPTION AND NUTRITIONAL GOALS IN AGRICULTURAL RESEARCH AND DEVELOPMENT

There are at least four steps that are crucial for addressing nutritional concerns in agricultural research and development. These relate to (1) the nutritional targeting of projects, (2) determining the acceptability of new crops and foods, (3) understanding the relationships between existing farming systems and nutrition systems, and (4) including food consumption and nutritional status in the monitoring and evaluation of projects.

Targeting

Targeting agricultural research toward groups at risk or the nutritionally neediest is a critical first step in incorporating nutrition into agricultural research and development projects. As Reutlinger (1983), among others, points out, agricultural and rural development projects often fail to reach those at greatest nutritional need. Targeting has been discussed by Mason (1983, 1984; Mason et al. 1985), Frankenberger (1985), and others. The process of targeting includes the identification of specific nutritional problems (either through surveys or use of secondary data), identification of groups at risk, and an analysis of the etiology of malnutrition that can be addressed through the implementation of agricultural research.

The nutrition planning literature includes an approach to targeting based on the identification of "functional classes"—the identification of groups at nutritional risk because they share common problems, ways of making a living, resource constraints, etc., and for whom a set of recommendations can be made. The notion of functional classification is parallel to the construction of "recommendation domains" (DeWalt 1985a) found in the application of a farming systems approach to agricultural research and development. A nutritional system analysis would include an identification of functional classes as part of an analysis of domains of application.

Studies of the effects of the Green Revolution (Griffen 1974; DeWalt 1979; Lipton and Longhurst 1985) have demonstrated that the package of technologies that performed the "miracle" favored farmers with greater resources and allowed, in some cases, for the further marginalization of resource-poor farmers and the landless (*see* DeWalt, this volume). That is, they were not scale-neutral technologies, nor were the credit and marketing policies that accompanied them scale-neutral. Lipton and Longhurst (1985) also conclude that the primary beneficiaries of the nutritional benefits of the Green Revolution (adoption of high-yielding varieties) were the urban poor rather than the rural poor. Lunven's analysis of several development projects, cited above, also points to a failure to tailor projects to the need of the farmers with the poorest resources. Those designing agricultural technology and promoting its implementation often argue that it is scale-neutral and that technology—i.e., new seeds, methods of cultivation, availability of credit, etc.—can be used profitably by farmers of all sizes. Omawale, reviewing a study carried out in Bangladesh, notes that

> it was concluded that a scale-neutral dairy-development project that brought some small immediate consumption benefits to the poor, would in the long run rebound to the disadvantage of resource-poor households since it presented a new opportunity for their exploitation, given the existing social relationships. On the other hand, it was found in the same study that a rural cooperative development project exclusively for the landless did confer a degree of independence on the participants in addition to immediate improvements in consumption. *In other words, scale neutral technology, although a welcome advance, may still be inadequate in situations in which the poorest need to be given special advantage.* (Omawale 1984:268, emphasis added)

Targeting also implies an understanding of the diet as a whole for the identification of problem areas—specific nutrients in short supply and the most acceptable dietary components to deliver those nutrients. Thus, targeting can provide the identification of nutritional problems, the selection of specific groups identified in terms of their nutritional needs and the constraints they face in meeting these needs, and the identification of crops and cropping techniques that can best address their needs.

Determining Acceptability of Interventions

The second area of investigation in the nutritional systems research framework focuses on the acceptability of crops or other foods—either newly introduced or whose availability would be increased through research. For example, the introduction of new, more productive varieties of food crops would have little impact on local diets if the varieties do not have the characteristics that make them acceptable as food, as in the case of hybrid sorghum in southern Honduras (DeWalt and DeWalt 1987), or if the variety was nutritionally inferior. Acceptability is closely tied to methods of food preparation and the kinds of products that result. The grain quality characteristics that produce an acceptable porridge may be different from those necessary for an acceptable flatbread or fermented beverage. In addition, preparation techniques may, in themselves, have an impact on the nutritional quality of food as in the relationship between the availability of niacin and alkaline treatment of maize (Katz, Hediger, and Valleroy 1975). Even though the relationships between indigenous preparation techniques and nutritional quality of a food may not be known, the introduction of new food crops without considering or anticipating the effects of preparation may promote a deterioration of dietary adequacy.

Communities may also have developed behavioral methods to minimize the harmful effects of some foods. For example, the use of fava beans in areas in which glucose-6-phosphate dehydrogenase deficiency is endemic may have been regulated through systems of belief about the appropriateness of fava beans for children and pregnant women, so that groups most at risk from the resulting hemolytic anemia were prohibited from using the beans (Katz and Schall 1979). An analysis of the acceptability and important organoleptic properties of food crops should include an understanding of the food beliefs and preparation practices surrounding the use of specific foods.

Linking the Farming System and the Nutrition System

The third research domain focuses on an understanding of the relationships between the existing farming and nutrition systems to anticipate the nutritional impacts of changes in technology. While a focus on the linkages outlined earlier may lessen the negative effects of new technology, any change in agricultural practices must take into account that the effects of introducing or modifying technology on the diets of households and regions are mediated through social processes such as changes in family organization, social structure, land tenure, marketing, etc. These may be anticipated in part through an analysis of the existing nutrition and social systems and through ongoing project monitoring.

Finally, all of these lines of research carried out at the inception of a research or development project can provide baseline data for the future evaluation of the effects of research. Data appropriate for evaluation of the impact of projects both on social organization and on the quality of life, as well as food consumption and nutrition, is too rarely available for adequate evaluation. Furthermore, project monitoring and evaluation designs rarely include the monitoring of food consumption and nutritional status.

CONCLUSIONS

As Valdes (1983) has pointed out, an agricultural policy does not imply a food policy. By the same token, agricultural and food policies do not imply a nutrition policy. The agricultural and food policies of many countries are directed toward goals that often compete with nutritional goals. Even when a nutrition policy is explicitly or implicitly included, the beneficiaries are often not those at greatest risk for nutritional deficiency. Our work over the last few years has been directed toward acting at the project level to explicitly include food consumption and nutrition goals for rural populations at risk in agricultural research and development. The approach outlined above has been developed as a guide to organizing research for project planning, implementation, monitoring, and evaluation. The key is that the processes that link agricultural production are mediated through social, cultural, and economic phenomena. Social and family organization, land tenure, traditional division of labor, and food beliefs and preferences are all crucial to understanding the ways that agricultural projects can affect the availability and consumption of food in the farm household and in developing interventions likely to have a positive impact.

NOTES

1. My work in Honduras (1981–83) and Mexico (1984) was supported by the International Sorghum and Millet Collaborative Research Support Project funded by the United States Agency for International Development (USAID). Work in Ecuador was supported by the Nutrition and Agriculture Cooperative Agreement with the Nutrition Economics Group USDA/OICD and the Office of Nutrition, Bureau of Science and Technology USAID, Washington.

The Food Game in Latin America

Paul L. Doughty

As food consumption in the industrial nations increases, Third World regions such as Latin America are increasingly pressed to maintain even their traditionally low levels of production and consumption—despite the vaunted "Green Revolution." Instead of rising levels of production because of the impact of new technology, food outputs in half of Latin America have actually fallen. This decline, the most serious in more than forty years, is part of a worldwide pattern which is cause of major concern.[1]

The United Nations (1989:36) attributes this decline to ecological deterioration, poor weather, shortage of land, and the diminishing returns of the "Green Revolution" in key nations. Although undeniably important, these reasons may gloss over other factors which demand attention, such as dramatic demographic changes, explosive population growth, and political crises abetted by ill-considered socioeconomic policies which cast their rippling effect downward through societies. The continuation of serious nutritional problems has raised questions about the impacts of international food programs and the continuing maldistribution of world supplies.

The impacts on families and communities of trickle-down governmental programs falls directly into the path of anthropologists who customarily work in this arena, far from the domains of economic analysts and development policy specialists who construct program guidelines to execute food policy decisions. Peasant farmers and urban squatters throughout the poorest countries of Latin America are often dependent upon and extensively influenced by the food programs of the United States and other nations. In the following pages we will follow the downward spiral of relationships between the Latin American populace and the agricultural and food policy of the "First World."

The asymmetrical nature of the political economies of the United States, Europe, and Japan with those of Latin American nations is one of patron to client, protector to ward, creditor to debtor, and welfare donor to beneficiary. This relationship is driven by the assumption that the United States could "feed the world"—accepted as a truism, if not a duty, especially when considered in light of the very real agricultural capacity and resources it enjoys. However noble the enterprise envisioned, doubts have nonetheless arisen about the effects of current U.S. food policy, particularly with respect to the influence it may have on foreign producers (Lappé, Collins, and Kinley 1980; Dunlop and Adamczyk 1983). Even assuming that the U.S. apportions its surplus food in a fair manner based upon need, additional questions may be raised regarding the ability of donor nations to arrange the adequate and equitable distribution of the food—across international boundaries and through the web of diverse social systems—without creating negative repercussions.

In this chapter I argue that U.S. food aid to Latin America is part of a giant ring that connects midwestern corn and wheat producers to Latin America's urban poor, peasant farmers, and immigrant farm laborers. Indeed, in the long run, these food policies may actually contribute to rather than solve the economic and political problems of some Latin American countries.

THE UNEVEN FIELD

During the past twenty-five years, the Latin American population has undergone a dramatic and widespread series of changes, brought on by relatively high yearly growth rates and large shifts in residence and employment patterns as millions migrated into the cities from provincial regions in each country (Table 1). Although the proportion of persons employed in agriculture remains more than 35 percent in ten Latin American countries, the numbers and percentages of persons engaged in agricultural pursuits have been steadily decreasing.[2] At the same time, the quantity of basic food imports purchased in the world market, mostly from the United States, has risen more than 50 percent. In addition to this increased dependency on a handful of exporting countries for essential foodstuffs, Latin America has witnessed a 210 percent rise in food assistance from all sources during 1975–1987, shifting substantially in country emphasis as well as total amount. The growth in all types of food imports has exceeded the 42 percent growth rate of total population by a substantial margin. Moreover, massive urbanization accompanied a 10 percent loss in the relative size of the agricultural labor force. Thus, agricultural production has not kept pace with either population growth or the changing demands of urban society.

On a per capita basis, the leading recipients of food aid in 1987 differ markedly from the ranking a decade earlier in both country and quantity of assistance offered. This fact reflects the changing political interests of the presidential administrations as much as actual food needs. Despite remarkable shifts in both emphasis and amounts of food imported, there has been no change in the estimates for daily caloric intake for the average Latin American in more than twenty years (World Bank 1988).

Although not the only supplier of basic food assistance, the United States is without question the dominant provider of food in both marketplace and in aid programs worldwide. In Latin America, American hegemony with respect to general food supply is overwhelming (Table 2). Indeed, the only country receiving a significant level of international food assistance which is not dependent on the United States is Nicaragua. As a result of the embargo placed on trade by the Reagan Administration, Nicaragua gets all of its supply from western Europe, Canada, and Argentina. In all other cases, U.S. food assistance constitutes more than 90 percent of all hemispheric food aid in all countries receiving it. The same dominance applies to commodity market sales as well.

United States Food Assistance to Latin America

The thirty-fifth anniversary of United States Public Law 480 (PL 480) was in 1989. Under this law thousands of metric tons of American-grown grains and other foods are annually sold to nations through the provisions of the two principal sections of the law—Title I and Title II. The first title permits governments to buy foodstuffs in local currency and retail market them through various mechanisms. Title II allows food to be distributed through Private Voluntary Organizations (PVOs) to alleviate disaster effects and confront endemic starvation and malnourishment through contracted programs such as maternal and child feeding and primary school meals.[3] In addition, PL 480 Title II encourages development activities through "food for work" projects in which

Table 1
Population, Food Imports, and Consumption in Latin America, 1965–1987

| Nation | 1987 Population | | Agriculture Labor | | GNP Per Capita 1987 | Average Daily Calorie Consumption (thousands) | | Cereal Imports (thousands of metric tons) | | Food Aid (thousands of metric tons) | | Food Aid per capita 1987 Rank |
	Number (millions)	Annual increase (%)	Percentage of Total Population 1980–87	Decline 1965–80 (%)		1965	1986	1974	1987	1975	1987	
Argentina	31.1	1.4	13	5	$2390	3.2	3.2	0	1	0	0	0
Bolivia	6.7	2.7	49	8	580	1.8	2.1	209	258	22	219	3
Brazil	141.4	2.2	26	17	2020	2.4	2.6	2485	3871	31	7	15
Chile	12.5	1.4	20	10	1310	2.5	2.6	1737	249	323	18	13
Colombia	29.5	1.9	34	11	1240	2.1	2.5	503	863	28	0	0
Costa Rica	2.6	2.3	27	16	1610	2.3	2.8	110	195	1	54	6
Dominican R.	6.7	2.4	24	14	730	1.8	2.4	252	683	16	117	8
Ecuador	9.9	2.9	36	16	810	1.9	2.0	152	347	13	53	11

El Salvador	4.9	1.2	40	16	860	1.8	2.1	75	182	4	247	2
Guatemala	8.4	2.9	58	7	950	2.0	2.3	138	284	9	193	5
Haiti	6.1	1.8	65	7	360	2.0	1.9	83	178	25	89	9
Honduras	4.7	3.6	53	7	810	1.9	2.0	52	178	31	137	4
Jamaica	2.4	1.4	26	6	940	2.2	2.5	340	412	1	333	1
Mexico	81.7	2.2	38	13	1830	2.6	3.1	2881	4797	0	4	15
Nicaragua	3.5	3.4	37	10	830	2.3	2.4	44	129	3	35	10
Panama	2.3	2.2	29	15	2240	2.2	2.4	63	116	3	1	12
Paraguay	3.9	3.2	47	6	990	2.6	2.8	71	2	10	2	14
Peru	20.2	2.3	35	10	1470	2.3	2.2	637	1894	37	237	7
Trinidad/Tobago	1.2	1.6	10	10	4210	2.4	3.0	208	282	0	0	0
Uruguay	3.0	0.5	17	4	2190	2.8	2.6	70	166	6	0	0
Venezuela	18.3	2.8	13	14	3230	2.3	2.5	1270	2003	0	0	0
Totals & avg.	401.0	2.2	33	10.5	1504	2.4	2.4	11380	17090	563	1746	

Sources: World Bank Development Report 1989; World Bank, *Social Indicators of Development 1988,* and Interamerican Development Bank, *Economic and Social Progress in Latin America 1989 Report.*

Table 2
Food Aid in Cereals from All Sources to Latin America, 1975–1986, and Major Donors, 1985/86

Nation	All Sources (thousands of metric tons)			Major Donors, 1985/6 (thousands of metric tons)				
	1975–76	1980–81	1985–86	Argentina	Canada	EEC Agencies	France	United States
Bolivia	8.0	54.7	292.5	.0	.2	23.0	.0	279.3
Brazil	3.0	3.0	5.6	.0	5.6	.0	.0	.0
Colombia	26.0	5.4	5.7	.0	5.7	.0	.0	.0
Costa Rica	1.3	.9	118.6	.0	.6	.0	.0	118.0
Domin Rep.	23.5	73.2	124.8	1.5	.0	2.0	2.0	121.3
Ecuador	6.4	9.0	4.7	.0	.0	.0	.0	4.7
El Salvador*	4.0	49.5	278.1	.0	1.1	8.6	.0	269.5
Guatemala+	16.8	13.9	52.5	.0	.3	4.7	.0	48.6
Haiti<	29.3	83.6	132.5	.0	.4	30.4	11.0	127.5
Honduras	13.4	35.8	135.0	.0	6.8	1.4	.0	127.5
Jamaica	6.4	37.2	202.5	.0	.3	.5	.5	201.6
Mexico>	.0	.0	10.8	.0	5.6	3.4	.0	3.3
Nicaragua**	3.1	58.3	40.6	10.0	9.8	27.6	11.0	.0
Panama	2.0	2.3	.4	.0	.0	.0	.0	.0
Paraguay	.1	10.9	3.7	.0	2.9	.0	.0	.4
Peru++	28.7	115.9	180.2	.0	.0	3.0	.0	177.2
Totals	172.0	553.6	1588.2	11.5	39.3	104.6	24.5	1479.7

Other food donors: (*) Norway and Switzerland; (+) the Netherlands; (<) West Germany; (>) the Netherlands; (**) Spain and Switzerland; (++) Spain. Source: FAO, Food Aid in Figures, 1987.

workers are paid in food allotments as an inducement for work done on community infrastructure projects.

Viewed in context of all food imports, PL 480 supplies are a significant factor in the recent history of Latin America, raising questions about the effectiveness and results of food assistance, particularly with regards to the long-term impact. In fact, at the very onset of the surge in food assistance programs under the Alliance for Progress, a Congressional oversight committee raised the question as to whether PL 480 would "affect" local markets or create what have come to be known as production "disincentives" (United States 87th Congress, Joint Economic Committee 1962:11). This remains an important question that is complexly enmeshed with specific attributes of a country's farm and market environment.

PL 480: Commerce Versus Humanitarianism

Although perhaps designed with vague humanitarian purposes in mind, the original PL 480 concept was more preoccupied with its political and economic functions, which specifically sought to increase U.S. commodity sales to friendly countries. The people-oriented character of the law did not emerge until the title "Food for Peace" was coined, reputedly by Senator Hubert Humphrey (Wallerstein 1980:180–85). The concept was subsequently developed by President Eisenhower and those who followed, raising its vision to larger purposes.[4] The few altruistic references in the law referring to disasters and relief work in greatly depressed regions (mostly in the Title II section) now received a wider scope for action. The first version of PL 480 made no mention of "development."

Despite changes in scope, the main goals of the law have always been the promotion of U.S. grain and food exports and the development of overseas markets for them—whether under PL 480 or commercial sales. In this endeavor, the law has succeeded. The tenfold rise in annual dollar value of all U.S. farm exports since 1954 (USDA 1981:1) is of critical importance for U.S. grain and dairy farmers. Moreover, the value of annual PL 480 programs under Titles I and II have increased more than three times since inception (USDA 1981: Table 1).

Food, Power, and Ideology

The fortunes of the PL 480 program have always been closely tied to perennially hot domestic issues: the U.S. farm policy and subsidy system, surplus grain management, foreign trade, and international relations. Each administration manages such issues with a different philosophy. For example, U.S. commitments to PL 480 dropped dramatically in the 1970s until the Carter administration, when the program share of agricultural exports rose from 4 to 11 percent of total value.

In spite of changes between administrations, PL 480 remains (after military aid) the most enduring aspect of U.S. foreign material assistance. PL 480 is an institution which serves the needs of many interests. As an intimate part of United States foreign policy, food aid lends itself to a carrot and stick approach that rewards friends and punishes enemies—providing an arena for continued or expanded operations for commodity traders and domestic farm groups while giving a scope to PVO programs that might not otherwise exist. Furthermore, PL 480 constitutes a major dimension of USAID's activities worldwide. State Department executives see food aid as food power, a tool to promote national political interests in critical context.[5]

The operations of PL 480 in a given country are related to the policy struggles that shape U.S. food assistance as well as to the situation in the recipient nation itself. Title I program foods funnelled through the marketplace are relatively difficult to trace and evaluate in terms of their primary and secondary impacts because they are not targeted at specific populations (Johnson et al. 1983; Dunlop and Adamczyk 1983).

Such is not the case for the implementation of Title II, the traditional Food for Peace division dedicated to the humanitarian concerns of hunger alleviation and the promotion of local level development. Expanded now to encompass development issues in direct fashion, Title II programs are faced with questions which are increasingly the subject for debate. These relate to the constant problems of determining just what constitutes "development" and defining the appropriate strategies for setting self-sustaining planned changes in motion. For example, USAID's use of local soft currency generated under Title I is governed by provisions in the law since 1967 to foster explicit self-help activities in the agricultural sector of recipient nations. These provisions

Members of a communal kitchen group receiving PL 480 food allotments, Peru. Photograph by P. Doughty.

include measures to increase lands under cultivation, encourage control of population growth, and generally improve farming and marketing.

Modifications made in the late 1970s sought to reemphasize the expansion of U.S. commodity markets *and* encourage local agricultural production and economic growth while avoiding competition with local products. Moreover, the monies generated from Title I food sales are destined to finance nutrition and development activities, encourage local organizations to handle PL 480 programs, evaluate for program effectiveness, use American experts to help local institutions implement programs, and achieve greater program continuity to receive multi-year funding (USDA 1981:1–27). The implications for food aid project activity in all recipient countries are therefore far reaching and could easily lead to unrealistic rhetorical claims or unreasonable expectations on the part of both donor and recipient.

FOOD EXPORTS AND POWER

The anomalies of world food production pose questions of fundamental importance to all countries but especially to those at the polar extremes in this regard. The most important foods are cereal grains, which provide more than 50 percent of all protein and calories consumed. Wheat, rice, corn, and barley along with soybeans and potatoes account for 77 percent of the major food crops (Food and Agricultural Organization [FAO] 1987a). Because of the importance of such crops as food, their distribution in production and consumption terms is critical.

The number of countries which export such staples is significantly small since most nations consume virtually their entire production, leaving little surplus for external markets. Only five countries (United States, Canada, France, Argentina, and Australia) are significant exporters of wheat, the world's most extensively cultivated and harvested crop. Less than 3 percent of the world's second largest crop, rice, is exported, yet five countries (China, India, Indonesia, Bangladesh, and Thailand) grow more than 70 percent of the total harvest. The United States, which grows only 1.5 percent of the total, is, surprisingly, the world's largest exporter of this staple. The remaining large-scale food staples—maize, barley, soybeans, and potatoes—are produced in similar patterns of nationally concentrated production. As a result, six nations (United States, U.S.S.R., China, Canada, India, and Brazil) account for most of the total basic food production. Of the leading producers of all the principal staples, only four (United States, Canada, Australia, Argentina) are significant exporters with no external food dependency (FAO 1987b:33–38), and only three of these are consistent suppliers of food through food assistance programs to Latin America— the United States being by far the largest donor (Table 2).

Thus the United States has great leverage in wielding its food power amongst needy nations and, indeed, has not hesitated to use it, as the Central American and other cases illustrate. To wit, Nicaragua was a relatively minor recipient of U.S. food aid until the time of the revolution in 1979, at which time U.S. PL 480 assistance increased by 157 percent only to be suddenly dropped the next year to virtually nothing and discontinued altogether the following year (U.S. House 1981:54). Not being a traditionally large food aid program, U.S. food support to Nicaragua was replaced by Canada, France, the European Economic Community, and Spain in all food categories, equaling the former U.S. contribution in most areas (Table 2).

Just as the United States moved militantly against Nicaragua in the wake of its social revolution, it also flooded the rest of Central America with enormous amounts of PL 480 supplies that were far in excess of anything these countries had heretofore received. In the case of Costa Rica, the increase rose from less than one to more than 118 metric tons in a year. The principal thrust of the Reagan Administration's economic assistance package was indisputably PL 480 food, not only in Central America but in such countries as Bolivia, Jamaica, and Peru as well.

This pattern will surely be observed as the U.S. and other western democracies rush to support the rapidly changing nations in the erstwhile Soviet Block of eastern Europe. We can predict with some confidence that the result will be less food available for Third World areas. Just as the United States throws money at political problems and opportunities, it also either throws food at them or takes it away.

The competition for basic food resources among nations acquires an ever keener edge, in which real need is not the principal criterion for determining who shall have access to world market supply. In fact, *all* of the lowest income groups of nations receive less per capita food from international sources than the wealthier countries, thus reconfirming

Terry Barr's assertion that "When shortfalls occur, the world market-place makes grain available to highest bidder; in the event of an extreme shortfall a developed country may limit exports. In either event, the lowest income countries are the least likely to acquire necessary supplies. . . . In addition, bilateral grain agreements serve to protect a significant share of available supplies for the more affluent countries, making the remaining market volume smaller and thus prices more volatile in years of reduced production" (Barr 1981).

An analysis of the distribution of foodstuffs according to national income categories shows that the neediest, least-developed nations have generally received the smallest portions of food aid resources, on a gross per capita basis. Middle-income nations have received the most. Furthermore, in the competition of the world food market, lower-income nations capture the smallest per capita share among all country groupings. Thus, in addition to Barr's theory, a corollary proposition is derived: the poorest countries do not command sufficient political interest on the part of the United States (or other donor nations) to attract consistently large or even average amounts of PL 480 support, despite demonstrable need or however friendly their political postures may be. Such countries attract food aid in substantial quantities on a per capita basis only when there is a political reward to be gained—as the cases of the Dominican Republic, El Salvador, Nicaragua, and Peru illustrate—or when a catastrophic event like the Sahelian drought focuses world attention on the tragedy of food scarcity.

Thus, the PL 480 program is not primarily humanitarian or developmental in character, rhetoric to the contrary. A review of the outcomes of the long history of food distribution indicates the variations among countries. Since the program began, Haiti received a total of $47 per each person alive by 1989. Although ranked as the twenty-ninth poorest nation on earth by the World Bank in 1987 and poorest in Latin America, Haiti has not benefited as much from PL 480 as its island neighbor the Dominican Republic which, ranking fifty-first as a lower-middle-income country, received an accumulated average of $70 per person (49 percent more per capita) in PL 480 assistance over the same period. Even more notably, Jamaica, ranked fifty-eighth in world income, received $140 per person in food assistance, the highest of any nation in the hemisphere and 61 percent more per capita than the second greatest recipient, El Salvador. Peru has received $29 per capita assistance in PL 480 food value for the thirty-five years.

All Latin American nations have received PL 480 assistance under either one or both Titles I and II in the past, although in 1988 seven were not obtaining these subsidies. Seen in perspective of thirty-five years, the U.S. per capita "investment" in the people of the region through food assistance and their related development projects is at once impressive, varied, and contradictory. The information in the tables may be surprising: few would guess that Chile, the Dominican Republic, and Costa Rica would rank so high as recipients of PL 480 resources while the impoverished Central American nations were historically among the lower half of beneficiaries.

It must also be noted and emphasized that PL 480, despite its prominent role in the U.S. foreign aid package, has not proven itself to be a successful instrument of development. When one looks at the countries that have been and are the recipients of food aid on a significant scale, there is little to be seen in the archives of accomplishment. It can be argued, and in fact demonstrated, that such programs as Food for Work contribute only tiny and often contradictory pieces to the massive puzzle of development (Doughty, Painter, and Burleigh 1984:160–253). In the end, reliance on such programs as a major portion of "development" assistance in Latin America is at best a Band-Aid and at worst a farce. In Bolivia, PL 480 constituted more than 50 percent of the USAID package in 1988 and 82 percent in 1980. In Peru, the percentages were 57 and 52 for the same years. As if this were not enough of a distortion in the development process, consider the capriciousness of the program from one year to the next when being in political favor determines both developmental fate and the extent of humanitarianism. The Manley administrations in Jamaica enjoyed relatively little support from the United States whereas the advent of the Seaga regime of the 1980s opened the PL 480 warehouse, making Jamaica the greatest per capita recipient of food aid in the hemisphere.

PERU: A CAUTIONARY TALE

A similar path can be traced in Peru, historically the second largest food assistance program in monetary terms for the region. How Peru with its rich resources and traditions reached its high level of food dependency is outlined briefly here for the light it sheds on this cautionary tale.

In the early 1950s, Peruvians began to exploit the country's vast fishery, catapulting the nation into world leadership in total tonnage. The anchovy fishery developed in response to world needs for inexpensive nutrients and fertilizer, and the coast of Peru was transformed virtually over night, from a collection of quaint postcolonial towns to a zone of intense growth with a frontier-like gold rush character. As peasants raced down from the Andes to become fishermen, the coastal cities—especially the capital of Lima—grew dramatically. Although there was some industrial growth in other areas of the economy, the true motor for the economic boom was fishing. The fishmeal of pulverized anchovy was bagged and sent around the world while Peruvian farmers watched their traditional guano supplies become more costly and scarce.[6]

Despite its great opportunity for agricultural development, Peru, like so many nations, followed the trends of the time, investing in urban development and hoping for industrial growth without commensurate attention to developing the rural and agrarian sectors of the society. Peru's farmers left the land, not because of mechanization or increased farm technology but because they saw opportunity in the urban areas and little in the rural. With its classic postcolonial social and political organization, archaic infrastructure, and deep ethnic divisions between the Indian highlands and the Spanish coast, Peru's economy lurched away from its past. Lima grew into a primate city, absorbing wealth and power from the rest of the nation. The countryside gave up its youth to urban growth. Rural areas remained stagnant.

In the mid-1950s, Peru experienced a severe three-year drought which resulted in a sudden increase in U.S. foreign assistance. After this, Peru became a regular recipient of bilateral assistance which focused on a nationwide school breakfast and lunch program and maternal and child health projects. The PL 480 program, as well as other aid, declined and disappeared after radical military revolutionaries assumed power in 1968, only to be restored again when conservative military forces assumed control of the government in the late 1970s. Renewed support reached a crescendo in the 1980s.

Despite early concerns with drought relief, the purpose of U.S. food policy in Peru has always been essentially political: "In Peru . . . the PL 480 Title I program was either renewed or significantly increased when it became possible not only to maintain democratically elected governments, but also to foster change via the election process towards a government with a more sympathetic view towards the United States. The renewal of PL 480 Title I assistance to Peru in 1978 helped stabilize the economy enough to permit national elections in 1980" (Dunlop and Adamczyk 1983:56–57).

Food imports have risen in unbroken fashion since 1947 as the government of Peru has attempted to reduce political instability by holding urban food prices down (Johnson et al. 1983:27–30). Despite the general intentions of PL 480 to assist the most needy, the main beneficiaries of these lower food prices appear to be the urban middle and upper classes (Johnson et al. 1983:32; World Bank 1989:223–24).

Indeed, some would argue that the large amounts of U.S. food aid to Peru have actually contributed to the downward spiral of rural underdevelopment. These lower food prices may have contributed to a shift in urban food preferences toward imported rice and wheat and away from traditional Andean staples produced by the rural smallholder (Ferroni 1980:36–37, 90; Johnson et al. 1983:30–33; World Bank 1989:223, 286). Since the Second World War, production of Peru's historic native staple, potatoes, has fluctuated and dropped on a per capita basis (Doughty 1986b).

In terms of economic and political development, the net effects of the substantial increase in U.S. investment in food aid in Peru have been ambiguous at best. By no means, however, can such unreliable support be equivalent to a development program. If food aid is to be truly used as part of a development scheme, then the consistency and measured use of it is critical. While evaluators had argued for the use of multi-year commitments of PL 480 in developmental contexts, there seems little likelihood that the kind of regularity required can emerge from the traditional political milieu of its employment. Serious doubt remains as to the proper role, if any, PL 480 can have in development other than in emergency and crisis situations.

Moreover, by temporarily relieving urban and population pressure for the development of national food self-sufficiency, food aid programs may have encouraged both Peru and the providers of government aid to focus attention on the production of exotic, nontraditional export crops, presumably to earn dollar income. For example, in the north central highland valley of the Callejón de Huaylas, a Miami-based German-American, with other farms in Peru and Columbia, operates a flower

Baking bread made from AID flour, Huaylas, Anchas, Peru. Photograph by
P. Doughty.

farm on the site of the old pre-earthquake (1970) airport on the banks
of the Santa river, not far from Vicos, site of the Cornell-Peru Project's
famous program in community development and land reform (Doughty
1987). Using the best irrigated midaltitude land which otherwise could
produce at least two food crops a year, this enterprise takes advantage of the "newly" paved road (after the 1970 earthquake) to ship
its delicate flowers via especially cooled vehicles to Lima and on to
the United States and Europe within twenty-four hours of picking. In
1983, I discovered that some of the then 300 workers in this operation regularly received PL 480 foodstuffs as part of Title II programs

in the area. Nearby, another extensive irrigated farm was operated by Japanese interests to grow marigolds whose brilliant blossoms were destined to be consumed by chickens so that their yolks would become sufficiently yellow for urban consumer tastes.

Having placed more than 50 percent of all its bilateral economic assistance to Peru over the last decade in the PL 480 food basket, the United States policy of encouraging friendly political stability through food power has little to show for the effort. Today the rural insurrection of the Sendero Luminoso guerrillas has affected more than 40 percent of the highlands. Impoverished rural farmers flock to the jungle to become coca suppliers, the national debt is extraordinary, and the government is in a state of political disarray. While U.S. foreign assistance policy does not own the exclusive rights to the current disaster, it must shoulder a prominent portion of the blame.

FOOD AID AND NONDEVELOPMENT IN LATIN AMERICA

To summarize, the lamentable decline in farm production and the failure to make significant progress in solving food shortages or increasing nutritional levels in many areas is the work of many factors: population growth, inequitable socioeconomic systems, urbanization, disaster, drought, and warfare. It is a web of variables woven together in a fabric of almost seamless quality.

Despite attempts to explain the perceived negative impacts of large-scale food assistance (Lappé, Collins, and Finley 1980:94–102; Stremplat 1981; Clay and Singer 1982:29–55; Dunlop and Adamczyk 1983), the statistically significant but inconclusive correlation between food assistance and a decline in food production from 1970 to 1981 in data from 79 Third World nations (Doughty 1986b:50) remains a nagging concern. This concern is especially pertinent when there is the massive use of food assistance employed as a political palliative or substitute for real long-term development programs.

It is unlikely that a single specific reason can account for production disincentives. Evaluations of PL 480 impacts in this regard have focused largely upon Title I, a macrolevel program whose detailed effects are lost in complex urban environments where PL 480 foods are largely distributed. In the case of Title II, however, the food is dispersed directly to beneficiaries and the impacts on these persons and families can be studied (Doughty, Burleigh, and Painter 1984). In the wide-ranging Food for Work programs in Peru, evaluators found that although food distribution was important in some areas, it did not detectably detract from farming. Moreover, when well-organized, Food for Work could obtain positive results in specific projects. But case studies also show that by paying people with food to work on community projects, the traditional willingness of people to undertake efforts for the community interest is often undermined, thus weakening local organization. Overall, however, such programs seemed but a small eddy of activity amidst a vast sea of need and demands for change.

The organization, scope, and consistency of general economic and social development activity is both puny and capricious. In Latin America's economic chaos of the 1980s, it was no wonder that analysts should suddenly discover hope in the "economy of desperation" now referred to as the "informal sector." However, the explosive development of agriculture's "informal sector"—coca farming—has brought no jog in a development sense despite production increases that surpass the Green Revolution.

The trends that we observed for Peru are increasingly visible throughout Latin America. The circumstances which contribute to declines in production and per capita food supply also encourage increased dependency on staple food imports (Table 3). Many Latin American countries such as Mexico, Costa Rica, and others have developed a growing beef export trade requiring grain imports as well as the use of local produce for feed (*see* DeWalt, this volume). At the same time, the PL 480 food package has emphasized wheat and, in some cases, rice which throughout the region can be characterized as urban staples. Indeed, these grains seem to be supplanting traditional native food staples such as potatoes and other tubers in the Andean countries and corn and beans in Mexico and Central America. Production of these classic staples has shown a steady decline throughout this decade, in some cases even resulting in the need to import them.

As this shift evolves, another change is also evident in the development of specialty farming in many countries: producing novelty items for export to the United States and Europe. Six Latin American countries, under international guidance, produce sufficient cut flowers of various types to undercut U.S. growers (U.S. International Trade Com-

Table 3

Agricultural Crop Production in Latin America, 1981–1986

Product	1986 (millions of metric tons)	Change from 1981 to 1986 (%)
Total cereals	107.2	2+
Wheat	21.5	41+
Rice	17.4	11+
Coarse grains	72.6	7−
Maize	52.8	4−
Barley	1.2	2−
Root crops	47.1	1+
Potatoes	11.4	3−
Pulses	5.0	7−
Vegetables & melons	19.3	18+

Source: FAO Production Yearbook, 1986. Vol. 40. Table 14 (1987).

mission 1986). Official encouragement of specialty exports as part of the United States's foreign assistance policy to Latin America is an ongoing policy illustrated by the visit to my university of a Guatemalan Maya village leader who was keenly interested in the prospects for artichoke production. With USAID assistance, his community would be on the cutting edge of this precariously dependent market. Additional forms of this new trade are also evident in the veritable explosion in the export of highly perishable vegetables and melons from Mexico, Central America, and the Caribbean to the United States (Stanford 1989), much in the tradition of the earlier banana trade from Central and South America (Adams 1914).

The problem confronting such specialized economic development is that these products must find and maintain a small niche in the metropolitan marketplace, coincide with seasonal scarcity and demand cycles, and provide the exacting quality and style required by fad-oriented urban purchasers in the importing nation. Third World producers such as those in Latin America might legitimately question the wisdom of making major investments under such circumstances— where they have little if any ability to understand the market and where they must operate under a buyers' monopoly that places all producers at a competitive disadvantage. In the case of Latin American perishable fruits and vegetables, single corporate buyers for massive food brokers and chains set conditions and prices on a take-it-or-leave-it basis: competition forces producers to lower their prices since the buyer is either alone or in collusion with other brokers across the border (Stanford 1989).

On the other side of this coin, lands which traditionally produced staple domestic crops such as corn or beans become enmeshed in investment, technology, and debt systems for the production of crops, which local persons do not use or need and which thus have little utility in the local or regional marketplace. It is hardly an atmosphere conducive to the development and empowerment of the rural poor in Latin America.

In nearby Latin American nations, both legal and illegal migration to the United States has reached a zenith, with a considerable portion of this population being employed in American agriculture: picking fruit and performing the undesirable low-paying labor required for harvesting many crops. Not including the illegal or temporary farm worker population or refugees, immigration to the United States from Latin America has increased by 21 percent in 1981–1987. Without foreign farm workers it is doubtful that south Florida's sugar cane, citrus, or a myriad of other crops elsewhere in the country could be harvested. American farmers have become fully dependent upon this agricultural labor to assist in achieving the national food surplus which exceeds all other nations. Ironically, the migrant farm workers who harvest these crops in the United States continue to live in poverty-ridden Third World conditions, underpaid and undernourished (Burns 1989:29–35).

The other dimension in the pattern of food dependency is on the supply side, where U.S. food producers are encouraged to fill Third World needs. We can hypothesize that because of this network of connections and the proclaimed objectives of PL 480, projects which would espouse food self-sufficiency and other locally oriented development plans that lessen the nature of food power as a political lever enjoy little popularity as large-scale, systematic strategies of international economic development. Such programs do not fit the models developed around the assumption that the major national producers of staple grains are destined to feed the world and profit from it.

Latin American farming communities are therefore directly affected as dependency relationships incorporate the individual directly into

the international system. Rural people thus become not only the consumers of the mechanized (value-added) food products but the producers of exotic (but low-cost) specialty crops, such as plantation crops
like sugar, tea, coffee, and bananas, for industrial urban markets in
metropolitan centers. They also enter the world system as part of the
international farm labor cohort which regularly migrates to the United
States to pick mass-produced crops and grains to be exported back to
the countries from which they come. The model is an old one, which
conjures up the colonial shadows and original effects of the industrial
revolution itself. Large-scale food aid is thus part of a great cycle of
asymmetrical economic relationships that work to the disadvantage of
Latin America's poor and thwart effective national development.

NOTES

I wish to acknowledge the assistance of Lois Stanford in assembling the
statistical data and reviewing some of the aspects of the food export economy
in Mexico and Michael Painter for our joint work on Peru.
  1. According to the United Nations World Economic Survey, 1989: "The
fall (in food production) was not only the largest ever recorded, but reduced
the world stock of cereals to below 17–18 percent of consumption that FAO
considers necessary for global food security." As a result of this decline and
notwithstanding technological advances, "the net food import requirements
for all food deficit developing countries are forecast to increase by some 70
percent by the end of the century . . ." (United Nations 1989:36–37).
  2. A word should be addressed to the issue of macrolevel statistics with
respect to their availability and correctness. The statistical material used in
this paper comes from the World Bank, Interamerican Development Bank,
FAO, the Encyclopedia Britannica Book of the Year, and various official U.S.
sources. Looking at these impressive annual compilations, it is easy to be
lulled into a sense of overconfidence as to their validity. In working with these
figures, however, questions inevitably arise which cannot be answered. For
example, the latest calculation of per capita GNP in 1965 of $390 shows a rise
to $1000 in 1975 and $1430 in 1987. From 1985 to 1987, the increase in GNP
per capita was 41%, and Peru vaulted from a World Bank ranking of 61 to 68,
passing Ecuador, Guatemala, Colombia, and Chile and drawing within shout-
ing distance of Costa Rica and Mexico! All of this has purportedly occurred as
the Peruvian economy has virtually collapsed because of violent insurrection,
its gargantuan debt, incompetent administration, a state of emergency cover-

ing half the country, and thousands of Peruvians seeking to leave for economic reasons. To anyone working in Peru, this ranking, the highest in history, must bring a reaction of incredulity. Similar surprises await review of nations such as El Salvador and Nicaragua. With misgivings, then, I have sought to analyze the available material, but readers must be forewarned that the statistical data only approximates a model of reality.

3. These include agencies such as CARE, Church World Service, and CARITAS. The World Food Program (WFP) of the United Nations also obtains most of its food supply from PL 480 and uses it in similar fashion.

4. John F. Kennedy, in particular, broadened the program scope as part of his foreign policy interests and to provide an action role for then up-and-coming George McGovern for whom the office of Director of Food for Peace was created.

5. This use of PL 480 is perennially strong, having inspired a brief change in name to "Food for Freedom" during the Johnson years (Wallerstein 1980:10), indicating the dominance of ideology over internationalist humanitarianism.

6. Guano is the dung of cormorants and other sea birds which feed on the shoals of anchovy and deposit their waste on the tiny off-shore islands from which guano has been mined for over five thousand years.

References

Aburto, H. 1979. El Maíz: Producción, Consumo, y Politica de Precios. In *Maíz: Politica Institucional y Crisis Agrícola*. Ed. C. Montañez and H. Aburto. Mexico: Editorial Nueva Imagen.

Adams, F. 1914. *Conquest of the Tropics: The Story of the Creative Enterprises Conducted by the United Fruit Company*. New York: Doubleday, Page and Company.

ADD Evaluation Unit. 1981 and 1982. Working Papers. Mimeographed. Blantyre, Malawi: Blantyre Agricultural Development Division.

Adelski, E. 1987. Ejidal Agriculture in Northern Sinaloa: Agricultural Resources, Production and Household Well-Being. Ph.D. diss., University of Kentucky.

Anderson, E., and M. Anderson. 1977. Modern China: South. In *Food in Chinese Culture*, ed. K. Chang. New Haven: Yale University Press.

Arizo-Nino, E., L. Hermon, M. Makinen, and C. Steedman. 1981. *Livestock and Meat Marketing in West Africa: Synthesis*. Vol. 1. Ann Arbor: University of Michigan, Center for Research on Economic Development.

Asante, S. 1986. Food as a Focus of National and Regional Policies in Contemporary Africa. In *Food in Sub-Saharan Africa*, ed. A. Hansen and D. McMillan. Boulder, Col.: Lynne Rienner Publishers.

Atherton, J. 1984. The Evolution of a Donor Assistance Strategy for Livestock Programs in Subsaharan Africa. In *Livestock Development in Subsaharan Africa*, ed. J. Simpson and P. Evangelou. Boulder, Col.: Westview Press.

Au Coin, D., M. Haley, J. Rae, and M. Cole. 1972. A Comparative Study of Food Habits: Influence of Age, Sex, and Selected Family Characteristics. *Canadian Journal of Public Health* 63:143–57.

Austin, J., and G. Esteva, eds. 1987. *Food Policy in Mexico: The Search for Self-Sufficiency*. Ithaca, N.Y.: Cornell University Press.

Baer, R. 1988. Consumption of Food Versus Other Wants and Needs: Household Level Strategies of Income Allocation and Food Consumption in Sonora, Mexico. Paper presented at the Meetings of the American Anthropological Association, Phoenix.

———. In press. Food Policy, Migration, and Malnutrition: The View from Northwestern Mexico. *Ecology and Food Nutrition*.

Barkin, D. 1982. El Uso de la Tierra Agrícola en México. *Problemas del Desarrollo* 47/48:59–85.

Barkin, D., R. Batt, and B. DeWalt. 1990. *Food Crops Versus Feed Crops: The Substitution of Grains in World Production.* Boulder, Col.: Lynne Rienner Publishers.

Barkin, D., and B. DeWalt. 1988. Sorghum and the Mexican Food Crisis. *Latin American Research Review* 23:30–59.

Barkin, D., and T. King. 1970. *Regional Economic Development in Mexico.* Cambridge and New York: Cambridge University Press.

Barkin, D., and B. Súarez. 1980. *El Complejo de Granos en México.* Mexico: Centro de Ecodesarrollo Serie Estudios 5.

———. 1982. *El Fin de la Autosuficiencia Alimentaria.* Mexico: Editorial Nueva Imagen.

———. 1983. *El Fin del Principio: las Semillas y la Seguridad Alimentaria.* Mexico: Océano.

———. 1986. *El Fin de la Autosuficiencia Alimentaria.* Mexico: Editorial Océano y Centro de Ecodesarrollo.

Barr, T. 1981. The World Food Situation and Global Grain Prospects. *Science* 214:1087–95.

Baxter, P. 1975. Some Consequences of Sedentarization for Social Relationships. In *Pastoralism in Tropical Africa,* ed. T. Monod. London: Oxford University Press.

———. 1979. Boran Age-sets and Warfare. In *Warfare Among East African Herders,* ed. K. Fukui and D. Turton. Senri Ethnology Series No. 3. Osaka: National Museum of Ethnology.

Beaton, G., and H. Ghassemi. 1979. *Supplementary Feeding Programs for Young Children in Developing Countries.* New York: United Nations Children's Fund.

Behnke, R. 1985. Measuring the Benefits of Subsistence Versus Commercial Livestock Production in Africa. *Agricultural Systems* 16:109–35.

———. 1988. Range Enclosure in Somalia. Pastoral Development Network Paper No. 25b. London: Overseas Development Institute.

Beneria, L., and M. Roldan. 1987. *The Crossroads of Class and Gender.* Chicago: University of Chicago Press.

Berg, A. 1972. Industry's Struggle with World Malnutrition. *Harvard Business Review* 50:130–41.

———. 1973. The Nutrition Factor. Washington, D.C.: Brookings Institution.

Blumenfeld, S., et al. 1982. Pl 480 Title II: A Study of the Impact of a Food Assistance Program in the Philippines. USAID Evaluation Report No. 6. Bureau For Asia. Washington, D.C.: USAID.

Boletin Interno (Dirección General de Economía Agrícola). 1982a. *Información Economica Nacional* 9, no. 1 (6 January).

Boletin Interno (Dirección General de Economía Agrícola). 1982b. *Información Economica Nacional* 9, no. 1 (11 August).

Boletin Interno (Dirección General de Economía Agrícola). 1982c. *Información Economica Nacional* 9, no. 1 (29 September).

Borlaug, N. 1983. Contributions of Conventional Plant Breeding to Production. *Science* 219:689–93.

Bouis, H., K. DeWalt, E. Kennedy, P. Pinstrup-Andersen, I. Nieves, and J. Braun. 1985. Conceptual Framework for a Research Network on the Income and Nutrition Effects of Increasing Commercialization of Semi-Subsistence Agriculture. Mimeographed. Washington, D.C.: International Food Policy Research Institute.

Braun, J. 1988. Effects of Technological Change in Agriculture on Food Consumption and Nutrition: Rice in a West African Setting. *World Development* 16:1083–98.

Braun, J., and E. Kennedy. 1986. *Commercialization of Subsistence Agriculture: Income and Nutritional Effects in Developing Countries.* Washington, D.C.: International Food Policy Research Institute.

Brown, L. 1971. The Biology of Pastoral Man as a Factor in Conservation. *Biological Conservation* 3:93–100.

Burgess, A., and R. Dean. 1962. *Malnutrition and Food Habits.* London: Tavistock Publications.

Burns, A. 1989. Immigration, Ethnicity and Work in South Florida. Occasional Paper No. 8. Gainesville, Fla.: Center for Latin American Studies, University of Florida.

Butterworth, D., and J. Chance. 1981. *Latin American Urbanization.* New York: Cambridge University Press.

Caballero, J. 1984. Agriculture and the Peasantry Under Industrialization Pressures: Lessons from the Peruvian Experience. *Latin American Research Review* 19:3–42.

Caballero, J., and E. Alvarez. 1980. Aspectos Cuantitativos de la Reforma Agraria (1969–1979). Lima: Instituto de Estudios Peruanos.

Centro de Estudios de Planeación Agropecuaria (CESPA). 1982. *El Desarrollo Agropecuario de México: pasado y perspectivas.* 13 vols. Mexico: Secretaría de Agricultura y Recursos Hidráulicos, Subsecretaría de Planeación.

Chambers, R. 1983. *Rural Development: Putting the Last First.* London: Longman Press.

Chavez, A. 1982. *Perspectivas de la Nutrición en México.* Publicación L-50. Tlalpan, Mexico: Instituto Nacional de la Nutrición.

Clark, B. 1975. The Work Done by Rural Women in Malawi. *Eastern African Journal of Rural Development* 8:50–91.

Clay, E., and H. Singer. 1982. Food Aid and Development: the Impact and Effectiveness of Bilateral PL 480 Title I-Type Assistance. USAID Program Evaluation Discussion Paper No. 15. Washington, D.C.: USAID.

Collinson, M. 1982. Farming Systems Research in Eastern Africa: The Experience of CIMMYT and Some National Research Services, 1975–1981. International Development Paper No. 3. East Lansing: Department of Agricultural Economics, Michigan State University.

Cornelius, W., and R. Kemper, eds. 1975. *Metropolitan Latin America: the Challenge and the Response.* Beverly Hills: Sage Publications.

Coughenour, M., J. Ellis, D. Swift, D. Coppock, K. Galvin, J. McCabe, and T. Hart. 1985. Energy Extraction and Use in a Nomadic Pastoral Ecosystem. *Science* 230:619–25.

Coughenour, M., and S. Nazhat. 1985. *Recent Changes in Villages and Rainfed Agriculture in Northern Central Kordofan: Communication Process and Constraints.* Report No. 4. Lexington, Ky.: INTSORMIL/University of Kentucky, College of Agriculture.

Coughenour, M., and E. Reeves. 1989. Social Science in INTSORMIL's Attack on Hunger in Sudan. In *The Social Sciences International Agricultural Research,* ed. C. McCorkle. Boulder, Col.: Lynne Rienner Publishers.

Couriel, A. 1984. Poverty and Underemployment in Latin America. *CEPAL Review* 24:39–62.

Cussler, M., and M. de Give. 1942. The Effect of Human Relations on Food Habits in the Rural Southeast. *Applied Anthropology* 1:13–18.

Dahl, G. 1979. *Suffering Grass: Subsistence and Society of Waso Borana.* Stockholm: Stockholm Studies in Social Anthropology.

Dahl, G., and A. Hjort. 1976. *Having Herds: Pastoral Herd Growth and Household Economy.* Stockholm: Stockholm Studies in Social Anthropology.

Department of Agricultural Research Crop Storage Research Section. 1980. Annual Report 1979/80. Chitedze, Malawi: Department of Agricultural Research.

de Haan, C. 1983. Towards a Framework for Pastoral Systems Research. In *Pastoral Systems Research in Sub-Saharan Africa: Proceedings from a Conference.* Addis Ababa: International Livestock Center for Africa (ILCA).

de Janvry, A. 1981. *The Agrarian Question and Reformism in Latin America.* Baltimore and London: Johns Hopkins University Press.

den Hartog, A., and A. Bornstein-Johansson. 1976. Social Science, Food, and Nutrition. In *Development from Below: Anthropologists and Development Situations,* ed. D. Pitt. The Hague: Mouton Publications.

Devadas, R. 1970. Social and Cultural Factors Influencing Malnutrition. *Journal of Home Economics* 62:164–71.

DeWalt, B. 1979. *Modernization in a Mexican Ejido: A Study in Economic Adaptation.* New York: Cambridge University Press.

———. 1985a. Anthropology, Sociology and Farming Systems Research. *Human Organization* 44:106–14.

———. 1985b. Mexico's Second Green Revolution: Food for Feed. *Mexican Studies/Estudios Mexicanos* 1:29–60.

———. 1988. Halfway There: Social Science *in* Agricultural Development and the Social Science *of* Agricultural Development. *Human Organization* 47:343–53.

DeWalt, B., and D. Barkin, 1987. Seeds of Change: The Effects of Hybrid Sorghum and Agricultural Modernization in Mexico. In *Technology and Social Change,* 2d ed., ed. H. Bernard and P. Pelto. Prospect Heights, Ill.: Waveland Press.

DeWalt, B., and K. DeWalt. 1980. Stratification and Decision Making in the Use of New Agricultural Technology. In *Agricultural Decision Making,* ed. P. Barlett. New York: Academic Press.

———. 1982. Socioeconomic Constraints to the Production, Distribution and Consumption of Sorghum in Southern Honduras. INTSORMIL, Farming Systems Research in Southern Honduras. Report No. 1. Lexington: University of Kentucky Experiment Station.

DeWalt, K. 1981. Diet as Adaptation: The Search for Nutritional Strategies. *Federation Proceedings* 40:2606–10.

———. 1983a. *Nutritional Strategies and Agricultural Change.* Ann Arbor: UMI Research Press.

———. 1983b. Income and Dietary Adequacy in an Agricultural Community. *Social Science and Medicine* 17:1877–86.

———. 1987. Case Studies in Nutrition and Agriculture. Technical Report No. 2. Cooperative Agreement for Nutrition and Agriculture. Office of Arid Land Studies, University of Arizona.

DeWalt, K., and B. DeWalt. 1987. Nutrition and Agricultural Change in Southern Honduras. *Food and Nutrition Bulletin* 9:36–45.

DeWalt, K., B. DeWalt, J. Escudero, and D. Barkin. 1988. The Nutrition Effects of Shifts from Maize to Sorghum Production in Four Mexican Communities. Paper presented in the symposium Cash Cropping and Nutrition held during the 14th Session of the United Nations Administrative Committee on Coordination-Subcommittee on Nutrition, Geneva, Switzerland, February 22 and 23, 1988.

DeWalt, K., and G. Pelto. 1977. Food Use and Household Ecology in a Mexican Community. In *Nutrition and Anthropology in Action,* ed. T. Fitzgerald. The Hague: Van Gorcum.

DeWalt, K., J. Uquillas, and C. Crissman. 1989. *Potatoes in the Food System of Highland Ecuador.* NEG/TA/OICD/USDA, Washington, D.C.: U.S. Department of Agriculture.

Dewey, K. 1980. The Impact of Agricultural Development on Child Nutrition in Tabasco, Mexico. *Medical Anthropology* 4:21–54.

———. 1981a. Nutritional Consequences of the Transformation from Subsistence to Commercial Agriculture in Tabasco, Mexico. *Human Ecology* 9:151–87.

———. 1981b. Agricultural Development, Diet and Nutrition. *Ecology of Food and Nutrition* 8:265–73.

Dirección General de Economía Agrícola (DGEA). 1980. Panorama Sobre El Comportamiento del Sector Agropecuario National 1977–1979 y Algunas Consideraciones sobre el Mercado Internacional. *Econotecnia Agrícola* 4.

———. 1982. Consumos Aparentes de Productos Pecuarios 1972–1981. *Econotecnia Agrícola* 6.

———. 1983a. *Información Agropecuario* 82.

———. 1983b. La Producción de Granos Basicos en México Estudio de sus Tendencias Recientes, sus Causas, y Perspectivas. *Econotecnia Agrícola* 7.

Doornbos, M., and M. Lofchie. 1971. Ranching and Scheming: A Case Study of the Ankole Ranching Scheme. In *The State of the Nations: Constraints of Development in Independent Africa,* ed. M. Lofchie. Berkeley: University of California Press.

Doughty, P. 1976. Social Policy and Urban Growth. In *Peruvian Nationalism,* ed. D. Chaplin. New Brunswick: Transaction Books.

———. 1979. A Latin American Specialty in the World Context: Urban Primacy and Cultural Colonialism in Peru. *Urban Anthropology* 8:383–98.

———. 1986a. Directed Culture Change and the Hope for Peace. In *Peace and War: Cross Cultural Perspectives,* ed. R. Rubinstein and M. Foster. New Brunswick: Transaction Books.

———. 1986b. Peace, Food and Equity in Peru. *Urban Anthropology* 15.

———. 1987. Against the Odds: Collaboration and Development at Vicos. In *Collaborative Research and Social Change: Applied Anthropology in Action,* ed. D. Stull and J. Schensul. Boulder, Col.: Westview Special Studies in Applied Anthropology.

Doughty, P., E. Burleigh, and M. Painter. 1984. Peru: An Evaluation of P.L. 480 Title II Food Assistance. Washington, D.C.: USAID.

Dunlop, D., and C. Adamczyk. 1983. A Comparative Analysis of Five PL 480 Title I Impact Evaluation Studies. USAID Program Evaluation Discussion Paper No. 19. Washington, D.C.: USAID.

Dwyer, D. 1983. Women and Income in the Third World: Implications for Policy. Working Paper No. 18. New York: The Population Council.

Dyson-Hudson, N. 1966. *Karamojong Politics.* Oxford: Clarendon Press.

————. 1986. Pastoral Production Systems and Livestock Development Projects: An East African Perspective. In *Putting People First: Sociological Variables in Rural Development,* ed. M. Cernea. Oxford: Oxford University Press.

Dyson-Hudson, R., and J. McCabe. 1985. *South Turkana Nomadism: Coping with an Unpredictably Varying Environment.* Ethnography Series FL17-001. New Haven: HRAFlex Books.

Edwards, K., G. Classen, and E. Schroten. 1983. *The Water Resources in Tropical Africa and its Exploitation.* ILCA Research Report No. 6. Addis Ababa: ILCA.

Eguren, F. 1980. Politica Agraria vs. Producción de Alimentos. *Quehacer* 3 (March):34–41.

Eicher, C., and D. Baker. 1982. Research on Agricultural Development in Sub-Saharan Africa: A Critical Survey. MSU International Development Paper No 1. East Lansing: Department of Agricultural Economics, Michigan State University.

Ellis, J., K. Galvin, J. McCabe, and D. Swift. 1987. *Pastoralism and Drought in Turkana District: Kenya.* Oslo and Nairobi: Norwegian Agency for International Development.

Ellis, J., and D. Swift. 1988. Stability of African Pastoral Ecosystems: Alternate Paradigms and Implications for Development. *Journal of Range Management* 41:450–59.

Ensminger, J. 1984. Political Economy Among the Pastoral Galole Orma: The Effects of Market Intergration. Ph.D. diss., Northwestern University, Evanston.

Evangelou, P. 1984. Cattle Marketing Efficiency in Kenya's Maasailand. In *Livestock Development in Subsaharan Africa: Constraints, Prospects, Policy,* ed. J. Simpson and P. Evangelou. Boulder, Col.: Westview Press.

Evans-Pritchard, E. 1940. *The Nuer: a Description of the Modes of Livelihood and the Political Institutions of a Nilotic People.* Oxford: Clarendon Press.

Feder, E. 1977. *Strawberry Imperialism: An Inquiry into the Mechanism of Dependency in Mexico.* The Hague: Institute of Social Studies.

Felstehausen, H., and H. Diaz-Cisneros. 1985. The Strategy of Rural Development: The Puebla Initiative. *Human Organization* 44:285–92.

Ferroni, M. 1980. *The Urban Bias of Peruvian Food Policy: Consequences and Alternatives.* Cornell University, Latin American Studies Program Dissertation Series No. 87. Ithaca, N.Y.: Cornell University Press.

Finsterbusch, K., and C. Wolf. 1981. *Methodology of Social Impact Assessment.* Stroudsburg, Pa.: Hutchinson Ross Publishing Company.

Fitzgerald, T. 1976. Ipomoea batatas: The Sweet Potato Revisited. *Ecology of Food and Nutrition* 5:107–14.

Fleuret, P., and A. Fleuret. 1980. Nutrition, Consumption, and Agricultural Change. *Human Organization* 39:250–60.

Food and Agricultural Organization (FAO). 1987a. *Production Yearbook 1986.* Vol. 40. New York: United Nations.

————. 1987b. *Food Aid in Figures 1987.* New York: United Nations.

Frankenberger, T. 1985. *Adding a Food Consumption Perspective to Farming Systems Research.* Washington, D.C.: USDA, Nutrition Economics Group, Technical Assistance Division, Office of International Cooperation and Development and USAID, Bureau for Science and Technology, Office of Nutrition.

Fresco, L. 1984. Comparing Anglophone and Francophone Approaches to Farming Systems Research and Extension. Networking Paper No. 1, Farming Systems Support Project. Gainesville, Florida: International Programs in Agriculture.

Fresco, L., and S. Poats. 1986. Farming Systems Research and Extension: An Approach to Solving Food Problems in Africa. In *Food in Sub-Saharan Africa.* Boulder, Col.: Lynne Rienner Publishers.

Galaty, J. 1981. Land and Livestock among the Kenyan Masai: Symbolic Perspectives on Pastoral Exchange, Change, and Inequality. In *Change and Development in Nomadic and Pastoral Societies,* ed. J. Galaty and P. Salzman. Special issue of the *Journal of Asian and African Studies.*

Galaty, J., D. Aronson, P. Salzman, and A. Chouinard, eds. 1981. *The Future of Pastoral Peoples.* Ottawa: International Development Research Centre.

García Sordo, M. 1985. Insuficiente producción para satisfacer la demanda de proteínas de origen animal. *UnoMásUno* (January 9):8.

Gilbert, E., D. Norman, and F. Winch. 1980. Farming Systems Research: A Critical Appraisal. Rural Development Paper No. 6. East Lansing: Department of Agricultural Economics, Michigan State University.

Gilmore, J., et al. 1980. Morocco: Food Aid and Nutrition Evaluation. USAID Project Impact Report No. 8. Washington, D.C.: USAID.

Gittinger, J., J. Leslie, and C. Hoisington, eds. 1987. *Food Policy: Integrating Supply, Distribution and Consumption* Baltimore: Johns Hopkins University Press for the World Bank.

Goldschmidt, W. 1967. *Sebei Law.* Berkeley: University of California Press.

————. 1976. *The Culture and Behavior of the Sebei.* Berkeley: University of California Press.

————. 1981. The Failure of Pastoral Economic Development Programs in

Africa. In *The Future of Pastoral Peoples*, ed. J. Galaty, et al. Ottawa: International Development Research Centre.

Grandin, B. 1955. *The Family Herds: A Study of Two Pastoral Tribes in East Africa, the Jie and the Turkana*. London: Routledge and Kegan Paul Ltd.

————. 1983. The Importance of Wealth Effects on Pastoral Production: A Rapid Method for Wealth Ranking. In *Pastoral Systems Research in Sub-Saharan Africa: Proceedings from a Conference*. Addis Ababa: International Livestock Center for Africa.

————. 1986. Adding Community Level Variables to FRS: A Research Priority. Paper presented at the IIMI-Rockefeller Foundation Workshop on Social Science Perspectives on Managing Agricultural Technology, Lahore, Pakistan.

Greiner, T., and M. Latham. 1981. Factors Associated with Nutritional Status among Young Children in St. Vincent. *Ecology of Food and Nutrition* 10:135–41.

Griffen, K. 1974. *The Political Economy of Agrarian Change: An Essay on the Green Revolution*. Cambridge: Harvard University.

Gross, D., and B. Underwood. 1971. Technological Change and Calorie Costs: Sisal Agriculture in Northeastern Brazil. *American Anthropologist* 73:725–40.

Gulliver, P. H. 1955. *The Family Herds: A Study of Two Pastoral Tribes in East Africa: The Jie and the Turkana*. London: Routledge and Kegan Paul Ltd.

Guyer, J. 1980. Household Budgets and Women's Incomes. Working Paper No. 28. Brookline: African Studies Center, Boston University.

Hansen, A. 1982. Intercropping and Farming Systems in Three Areas of Malawi. In Proceedings and Materials from the Conference on Intercropping Research in Malawi, October 20, 1981, A. Hansen, ed. Mimeographed. Chitedze, Malawi: Agricultural Research Station.

————. 1984. Zambia, Farming Systems Research and the Anthropological Body of Knowledge. Keynote Address to the Networkshop on the Role of Rural Sociology (Including Anthropology) in Farming Systems Research, November 27–29, 1984, Lusaka, Zambia. Mimeographed.

————. 1986. Farming Systems Research in Phalombe, Malawi: The Limited Utility of High Yielding Varieties. In *Social Sciences and Farming Systems Research: Methodological Perspectives on Agriculture and Development*, ed. J. Jones and B. Wallace. Boulder, Col.: Westview Press.

Hansen, A., and D. McMillan, eds. 1986. *Food in Sub-Saharan Africa*. Boulder, Col.: Lynne Rienner Publishers.

Hansen, A., E. Mwango, and B. Phiri. 1982. Farming Systems Research in Phalombe Project, Malawi: Another Approach to Smallholder Research and Development. Gainesville, Florida: Center for Tropical Agriculture.

Hansen, A., and J. Ndengu. 1983. Lilongwe Rural Development Project Cropping Patterns and Information from the National Sample Survey of Agriculture. Paper presented at the Ministry of Agriculture, April 1983, Lilongwe, Malawi. Mimeographed.

Hansen, A. 1981. Farming Systems of Alachua County, Florida: An Overview with Special Attention to Low Resource Farmers. Gainesville: Center for Community and Rural Development, Institute of Food and Agricultural Sciences, University of Florida.

Hardin, G. 1968. The Tragedy of the Commons. *Science* 162:1243–48.

Hardy, C. 1982. Mexico's Development Strategy for the 1980s. *World Development* 10:501–12.

Harriss, B. 1979a. Going Against the Grain. *Development and Change* 10:363–84.

———. 1979b. There is Method to My Madness: Or is it Vice Versa? Measuring Agricultural Performance. *Food Research Institute Studies* 17:197–218.

Haugerud, A. 1988. Anthropology and Interdisciplinary Agricultural Research in Rwanda. In *Anthropology of Development and Change in East Africa*, ed. D. Brokensha and P. Little. Boulder, Col.: Westview Press.

Herman, L. 1979. The Livestock and Meat Marketing System in Upper Volta: An Evaluation of Economic Efficiency. Livestock Production and Marketing in the Entente States of West Africa, Monograph No. 4. Ann Arbor: Center for Research on Economic Development, University of Michigan.

Hernandez, M., C. Hidalgo, J. Hernandez, H. Madrigal, and A. Chavez. 1974. Effect of Economic Growth on Nutrition in a Tropical Community. *Ecology of Food and Nutrition* 3:283–91.

Hewitt de Alcantara, C. 1976. *Modernizing Mexican Agriculture*. Geneva: United Nations Research Institute for Social Development.

Hildebrand, P. 1984. Modified Stability Analysis of Farmer Managed On-Farm Trials. *Agronomy Journal* 76:271–74.

Hildebrand, P., and F. Poey. 1985. On-Farm Agronomic Trials in Farming Systems Research and Extension. Boulder, Col.: Lynne Rienner Publishers.

Hill, P. 1986. *Development Economics on Trial: The Anthropological Case for a Prosecution*. Cambridge: Cambridge University Press.

Hoben, A. 1979. Lessons from a Critical Examination of Livestock Projects in Africa. A.I.D. Program Evaluation Working Paper No. 26. Washington, D.C.: Aid for International Development.

Hopkins, R. 1987. The Evolution of Food Aid: Toward a Development—First Regime. In *Food Policy: Integrating Supply, Distribution and Consumption*, ed. J. Price Gittinger, J. Leslie, and C. Hoisington. Baltimore: Johns Hopkins University Press for the World Bank.

Horowitz, M. 1981. Research Priorities in Pastoral Studies: An Agenda for the Eighties. In *The Future of Pastoral Peoples*, ed. J. Galaty, D. Aronson, P. Salzman, and A. Chouinard. Ottawa: International Development Research Center.

————. 1986. Ideology, Policy and Praxis in Pastoral Livestock Development. In *Anthropology and Rural Development in West Africa*, ed. M. Horowitz and T. Painter. Boulder, Col.: Westview Press.

Horowitz, M., and P. Little. 1987. African Pastoralism and Poverty: Some Implications for Drought and Famine. In *Drought and Hunger in Africa: Denying Famine a Future*, ed. M. Glantz. Cambridge: Cambridge University Press.

Hyden, G. 1983. *No Shortcuts to Progress: African Development Management in Perspective*. Berkeley: University of California Press.

Instituto Nacional de Estadística, Geografía e Informática (INEGI). 1987. *El Sector Alimentario en México. 1986*. Mexico: Instituto Nacional de Estadística, Geografía e Informática.

International Institute of Tropical Agriculture (IITA). 1986. Round-table on Nutrition and Agriculture. Ibadan, Nigeria: IITA.

International Livestock Center for Africa (ILCA). 1979. Annual Report. Addis Ababa: ILCA.

————. 1987. Annual Report. Addis Ababa: ILCA.

Jacobs, A. 1965a. The Traditional Political Organization of the Pastoral Masai. Ph.D. diss., Oxford University.

————. 1965b. African Pastoralists: Some General Remarks. *Anthropological Quarterly* 38:144–54.

Jahnke, H. 1982. *Livestock Production Systems and Livestock Development in Tropical Africa*. Kiel: Kieler Wissenschaftsverlag Vauk.

Jennings, B. 1988. *Foundations of International Agricultural Research: Science and Politics in Mexican Agriculture*. Boulder, Col.: Westview Press.

Johnson, T., et al. 1983. The Impact of PL 480 Title I in Peru: Food Aid as an Effective Development Resource. USAID Project Impact Evaluation Report No. 47. Washington, D.C.: USAID.

Katz, S., M. Hediger, and L. Valleroy. 1975. Traditional Maize Processing Techniques in the New World: Anthropology and Nutritional Science. *Science* 184:765–73.

Katz, S., and J. Schall. 1979. Fava Bean Consumption and Biocultural Evolution. In *Nutrition and Behavior*, ed. W. Barker. Hartford, Conn.: AVI Press.

Kemp, W. 1971. The Flow of Energy in a Hunting Society. *Scientific American* 225:104–15.

Kennedy, E., and B. Cogill. 1988. The Commercialization of Agriculture and Household-level Food Security: The Case of Southwestern Kenya. *World Development* 16:1075–81.

Kennedy, E., and P. Pinstrup-Andersen. 1984. *Nutrition-Related Policies and Programs: Past Performances and Research Needs*. Washington, D.C.: International Food Policy Research Institute.

Klima, G. 1970. *The Barabaig: East African Cattle Herdsmen*. New York: Holt, Rinehart and Winston.

Knudson, O., and P. Scandizzo. 1979. *Nutrition and Food Needs in Developing Countries*. World Bank Staff Working Paper No. 328. Washington, D.C.: World Bank.

Kumar, S. 1978. Role of the Household Economy in Child Nutrition at Low Incomes. Occasional Paper No. 95. Ithaca: Department of Agricultural Economics, Cornell University.

Lamprey, H. 1983. Pastoralism Yesterday and Today: The Overgrazing Problem. In *Ecosystems of the World 13: Tropical Savannas*. Ed. F. Bourliere. Amsterdam: Elsevier Scientific Publishing Co.

Lappé, F., J. Collins, and D. Kinley. 1980. Aid As Obstacle: Twenty Questions About Our Foreign Aid and the Hungry. San Francisco: Institute for Food and Development Policy.

Latham, M. 1984. Strategies for the Control of Malnutrition and the Influence of the Nutritional Sciences. *Food and Nutrition* 10:5–32.

Legesse, A. 1973. *Gada: Three Approaches to the Study of African Society*. New York: Free Press.

Lele, U. 1979. *The Design of Rural Development: Lessons from Africa*. Baltimore: Johns Hopkins University Press for the World Bank.

Linowitz, S. 1980. Overcoming World Hunger: The Challenge Ahead. Report of the Presidential Commission on World Hunger. Washington, D.C.

Lipton, M., and R. Longhurst. 1985. *Modern Varieties, International Agriculture Research, and the Poor*. CGIAR Study Paper No. 2. Washington, D.C.: The World Bank.

Little, P. 1985. Absentee Herdowners and Part-time Pastoralists: The Political Economy of Resource Use in Northern Kenya. *Human Ecology* 13:131–51.

Livingstone, I. 1977. Economic Irrationality Among Pastoral Peoples: Myth or Reality. *Development and Change* 8:209–30.

Longhurst, R. 1983. Agricultural Production and Food Consumption: Some Neglected Linkages. *Food and Nutrition* 9:2.

———. 1988. Cash Crops, Household Food Security and Nutrition. *IDS Bulletin*. April 1988.

Lunven, P. 1982. The Nutritional Consequences of Agricultural Development and Rural Development Projects. *Food and Nutrition Bulletin* 4:17–22.

Manger, L., ed. 1984. *Trade and Traders in the Sudan*. Bergen Occasional Papers in Social Anthropology No. 32. Bergen, Norway: Department of Social Anthropology, University of Bergen.

Marchione, T. 1980. Factors Associated with Malnutrition in the Children of Western Jamaica. In *Nutritional Anthropology,* ed. N. Jerome, R. Kandel, and G. Pelto. Pleasantville, N.Y.: Redgrave Publishing Company.

Mason, J. 1983. Minimum Data Needs for Assessing the Nutritional Effects of Agriculture in Rural Development Projects. In *Nutritional Impact of Agricultural Projects, Papers and Proceedings of a Workshop Held by the United Nations Inter-Agency Sub-Committee on Nutrition,* ed. J. Muscat. Rome: International Fund for Agricultural Development.

———. 1984. *Data Needs for Assessing the Nutritional Effects of Agricultural and Rural Development Projects: A Paper for Project Planners. Nutrition in Agriculture No. 4.* Rome: Food and Agriculture Organization of the United Nations.

Mason, J., M. Garcia, J. Mitchell, K. Test, C. Henderson, and H. Tabatabai. 1985. Nutritional Considerations in Project Planning: A Case Study of Assessment Methods. *Food Policy* (May):109–22.

Maxwell, S. 1988. The Nutrition Effects of Cash Crops. Paper presented in the symposium Cash Cropping and Nutrition held during the 14th Session of the United Nations Administrative Committee on Coordination, Subcommittee on Nutrition, Geneva, Switzerland, February 22 and 23, 1988.

Maxwell, S., and A. Fernando. 1988. *Cash Crops in Developing Countries: The Issues, the Facts, the Policies.* Sussex: The Institute for Development Studies.

McCabe, J. 1985. Livestock Management among the Turkana: A Social and Ecological Analysis of Herding in an East African Pastoral Population. Ph.D. diss., State University of New York, Binghamton.

———. 1987a. Drought and Recovery: Livestock Dynamics among the Ngisonyoka Turkana of Kenya. *Human Ecology* 15:371–89.

———. 1987b. Inter-Household Variation in Livestock Production in Southern Turkana District, Kenya. *Journal of Research in Economic Anthropology* 8:277–93.

———. 1988. Turkana Pastoralism: A Case Against the Tragedy of the Commons. Paper presented at the Twelfth International Congress of Anthropological and Ethnological Sciences, Zagreb, Yugoslavia. July 1988.

McCabe, J., J. Ellis, and T. Hart. 1984. *Impact of the Kapunguria-Lodwar Road.* Nairobi: Final Report to the Norwegian Agency for International Development.

McDowell, R. 1984. Livestock Nutrition in Subsaharan Africa: An Overview. In *Livestock Development in Subsaharan Africa: Constraints, Prospects, Policy,* ed. J. Simpson and P. Evangelou. Boulder, Col.: Westview Press.

McKenzie, J. 1974. The Impact of Economic and Social Status on Food Choice. *Proceedings of the Nutritional Society* 33:67–73.

McLean, W. 1987. Nutritional Risk: Concepts and Implications. In *Food Policy: Integrating Supply, Distribution and Consumption,* ed. J. Price Gittinger, J. Leslie, and C. Hoisington. Baltimore: Johns Hopkins University Press for the World Bank.

Mead, M. 1953. Cultural Patterns and Technical Change. Paris: UNESCO.

Meadows, S., and J. White. 1979. Structure of Herds and Determinants of Offtake Rates in Kajiadio District, Kenya. *ODI Pastoral Development Paper No. 7d.* London: Overseas Development Institute.

Meissner, F. 1981. The Mexican Food System (SAM): A Strategy for Sowing Petroleum. *Food Policy* 6:219–30.

Messer, E. 1972. Patterns of "Wild" Plant Consumption in Oaxaca, Mexico. *Ecology of Food and Nutrition* 1:325–32.

————. 1977. The Ecology of a Vegetarian Diet in a Modernizing Mexican Community. In *Nutrition and Anthropology in Action,* ed. Thomas K. Fitzgerald. Assen: van Gorcum.

Migot-Adholla, S., and P. Little. 1981. The Evolution of Policy Toward the Development of Pastoral Areas of Kenya. In *The Future of Pastoral Peoples,* ed. J. Galaty, et al. Ottawa: International Development Research Centre.

Ministry of Agriculture. 1981. Guide to Agricultural Production in Malawi, 1981–1982. Lilongwe, Malawi: Extension Aids Branch.

Molina, S. 1983. Comments on Economic Growth, Income Distribution, and Human and Social Development in Latin America. In *Nutrition Intervention Strategies in National Development,* ed. B. A. Underwood. New York: Academic Press.

Moris, J. 1986. Directions in Contemporary Pastoral Development. *ODI Pastoral Network Paper 22a.* London: Overseas Development Institute.

National Statistic Office. 1982. Preliminary Report: National Sample Survey of Agriculture for Customary Land 1980/81. Zomba, Malawi: Government Printer.

National Statistical Office. 1970. National Sample Survey of Agriculture 1968/69. Zomba, Malawi: Government Printer.

Nietschmann, B. 1973. *Between Land and Water.* New York: Seminar Press.

Norman, D. W., E. B. Simmons, and H. M. Hays. 1982. *Farming Systems in the Nigerian Savanna: Research and Strategies for Development.* Boulder, Col.: Westview Press.

Okere, L. 1983. *The Anthropology of Food in Rural Igboland, Nigeria: Socioeconomic and Cultural Aspects of Food and Food Habits in Rural Igboland.* Lanham, Maryland: University Press of America.

Omawale. 1984. Incorporating Nutrition Concerns into the Specification of Desired Technology Characteristics in International Agricultural Research.

In *International Agricultural Research and Human Nutrition*, ed. P. Pinstrup-Andersen, A. Berg, and M. Forman. Washington, D.C.: International Food Policy Research Institute.

Oxby, C. 1981. *Group Ranches in Kenya*. Rome: Food and Agriculture Organization.

Painter, M. 1984. Changing Relations of Production and Rural Underdevelopment. *Journal of Anthropological Research* 40:271–92.

Pearse, A. 1980. *Seeds of Plenty, Seeds of Want: Social and Economic Implications of the Green Revolution*. New York: Oxford University Press.

Picardi, A., and W. Siefert. 1976. A Tragedy of the Commons in the Sahel. *Technology Review* 78:42–51.

Pines, J. 1983. The Nutritional Consequences of Agricultural Projects: Evidence and Response. In *Nutritional Impact of Agricultural Projects, Papers and Proceedings of a Workshop held by the United Nations Inter-Agency Sub-Committee on Nutrition*, ed. J. Muscat. Rome: IFAD.

Pinstrup-Andersen, P. 1981. *Nutritional Consequences of Agricultural Projects: Conceptual Relationships and Assessment Approaches*. World Bank Staff Working Paper No. 456. Washington, D.C.: World Bank.

———. 1983a. Estimating the Nutritional Impact of Food Policies: A Note on the Analytical Approach. Paper presented at the meeting of the International Congress of Anthropological and Ethnological Sciences, Vancouver.

———. 1983b. *Export Crop Production and Malnutrition*. Washington, D.C.: International Food Policy Research Institute.

Pinstrup-Andersen, P., A. Berg, and M. Forman, eds. 1984. *International Agricultural Research and Human Nutrition*. Washington, D.C.: International Food Policy Research Institute.

Pinstrup-Andersen, P., and E. Caicedo. 1978. The Potential Impact of Changes in Income Distribution on Food Demand and Human Nutrition. *Journal of Agricultural Economics* 60:402–15.

Pinstrup-Andersen, P., and P. Hazell. 1987. The Impact of the Green Revolution and Prospects for the Future. In *Food Policy: Integrating Supply, Distribution, and Consumption*, ed. J. Gittinger, J. Leslie, and C. Hoisington. Baltimore: Johns Hopkins University Press.

Pitner, J., J. Lazo de la Vega, and N. Durón, 1954. *El Cultivo del Sorgo*. Mexico: Programa Cooperativo de Agricultura y Ganaderia de México y la Fundación Rockefeller.

Plucknett, D., and N. Smith. 1982. Agricultural Research and Third World Food Production. *Science* 217:215–20.

Poleman, T. 1981. A Reappraisal of the Extent of World Hunger. *Food Policy* 6:236–52.

Popkin, B., and F. Solon. 1976. Income, Time, the Working Mother and Child Nutrition. *Journal of Tropical Pediatrics and Environmental Child Health* 22:156–66.

Pratt, D. 1984. Ecology and Livestock. In *Livestock Development in Subsaharan Africa: Constraints, Prospects, Policy,* ed. J. Simpson and P. Evangelou. Boulder, Col.: Westview Press.

Quinby, J. 1971. *A Triumph of Research: Sorghum in Texas.* College Station: Texas A & M University Press.

Raikes, P. 1981. *Livestock Development and Policy in East Africa.* Uppsala: Scandinavian Institute of African Studies.

Rama, R., and F. Rello. 1982. *Estrategias de las Agroindustrias Transnacionales y Política Alimentaria en México.* Mexico City: UNAM, Facultad de Economía.

Rama, R., and R. Vigorito. 1979. *El Complejo de Frutas y Legumbres en México.* Mexico: Editorial Nueva Imagen.

Rappaport, R. 1984. *Pigs for the Ancestors: Ritual in the Ecology of a New Guinea People.* New Haven: Yale University Press.

Read, M. 1964. The Role of the Anthropologist. In *Changing Food Habits,* ed. J. Yudkin and J. McKenzie. London: MacGibbon and Kee.

Reeves, E. 1984. *An Indigenous Rural Marketing System in North Kordofan, Sudan.* Report No. 3. Lexington: INTSORMIL/University of Kentucky, College of Agriculture.

——— . 1989. Market Places, Market Channels, Market Strategies: Levels for the Analysis of a Regional System. In *Human Systems Ecology: Studies in the Integration of Political Economy, Adaptation, and Socionatural Regions,* ed. S. Smith and E. Reeves. Boulder, Col.: Westview Press.

Reeves, E., B. DeWalt, and K. DeWalt, 1987. The International Sorghum/Millet Research Project. In *Anthropological Praxis: Translating Knowledge into Action,* ed. R. Wulff and S. Fiske, pp. 72–83. Boulder, Col.: Westview Press.

Reeves, E., and T. Frankenberger. 1981. *Farming Systems Research in North Kodofan, Sudan.* Report No. 1. Lexington: INTSORMIL/University of Kentucky, College of Agriculture.

Reeves, E., and T. Frankenberger. 1982. *Farming Systems Research in North Kordofan, Sudan.* Report No. 2. Lexington: INTSORMIL/University of Kentucky, College of Agriculture.

Reutlinger, Shlomo. 1983. Nutritional Impact of Agricultural Projects: Conceptual Framework. In Papers and Proceedings of a Workshop Held by the United Nations ACC Sub-Committee on Nutrition. Washington, D.C.: IFAD.

Rhodes, R. 1984. *Breaking New Ground: Agricultural Anthropology.* Lima: International Potato Center.

Rigby, P. 1969. *Cattle and Kinship among the Gogo: A Semi Pastoral Society of Central Tanzania.* Ithaca: Cornell University Press.

Roberts, K. 1982. Agrarian Structure and Labor Mobility in Rural Mexico. *Population and Development Review* 8:299–322.

————. 1985. Technology Transfer in the Mexican Bajio: Seeds, Sorghum and Socioeconomic Change. In *Regional Aspects of U.S.-Mexican Integration,* ed. R. Anzaldua and I. Rosenthal-Urey, La Jolla: Center for U.S.-Mexican Studies, University of California, San Diego.

Rockefeller Foundation. 1957. *Mexican Agricultural Program, 1956–1957: Director's Annual Report.* New York: Rockefeller Foundation.

Rogers, E. 1971. *Communication of Innovations: A Cross-Cultural Approach.* Toronto: Collier-Macmillan.

Rutlinger, S. 1983. Nutritional Impact of Agricultural Projects: Conceptual Framework. In *Papers and Proceedings of a Workshop Held by the United Nations ACC Sub-Committee on Nutrition.* Washington, D.C.: IFAD.

Sanderson, S. Walsh. 1984. *Land Reform in Mexico: 1910–1980.* New York: Academic Press.

Sanderson, S. 1986. The Emergence of the "World Steer": International and Foreign Domination in Latin American Cattle Production. In *Food, The State and International Political Economy: Dilemmas of Developing Countries,* ed. F. Tullis and W. Hollist, pp. 123–48. Lincoln: University of Nebraska Press.

Sandford, S. 1983. *Management of Pastoral Development in the Third World.* London: John Wiley and Sons, in association with the Overseas Development Institute.

Saul, M. 1987. The Organization of a West African Grain Market. *American Anthropologist* 89:74–95.

Schneider, H. 1957. The Subsistence Role of Cattle Among the Pakot and in East Africa. *American Anthropologist* 59:278–300.

Selowsky, M. 1979. Balancing Trickle Down and Basic Needs Strategies: Income Distribution Issues in Large Middle-Income Countries with Special Reference to Latin America. World Bank Staff Working Paper No. 335. Washington, D.C.: World Bank.

Sen, A. 1987. Poverty and Entitlements. In *Food Policy: Integrating Supply, Distribution and Consumption,* ed. J. Price Gittinger, J. Leslie, and C. Hoisington. Baltimore: Johns Hopkins University Press for the World Bank.

Shaner, W., P. Philipp, and W. Schmehl. 1982. *Farming Systems Research and*

Development: Guidelines for Developing Countries. Boulder, Col.: Westview Press.

Sherman, J. 1981. *Crop Disposal and Grain Marketing in the Manga Region of Upper Volta: A Case Study.* Preliminary Working Paper. Ann Arbor: University of Michigan, Center for Research on Economic Development.

Sherman, J., K. Shapiro, and E. Gilbert. 1987. *The Dynamics of Grain Marketing in Burkina Faso: An Economic Analysis of Grain Marketing.* Vol. 1. Ann Arbor: University of Michigan Center for Research on Economic Development, with the University of Wisconsin.

Shils, E. 1981. *Tradition.* Chicago: University of Chicago Press.

Simic, A. 1973. The Peasant-Urbanites: A Study of Rural-Urban Migration in Serbia. New York: Seminar Press.

Simpson, J. 1984. Problems and Constraints, Goals and Policy: Conflict Resolution in the Development of Subsaharan Africa's Livestock Industry. In *Livestock Development in Subsaharan Africa: Constraints, Prospects, Policy,* ed. J. Simpson and P. Evangelou. Boulder, Col.: Westview Press.

Simpson, J., and P. Evangelou, ed. 1984. *Livestock Development in Subsaharan Africa: Constraints, Prospects, Policy.* Boulder, Col.: Westview Press.

Simpson, J., and R. McDowell. 1986. Livestock Economies of Sub-Saharan Africa. In *Food in Sub-Saharan Africa,* ed. A. Hansen and D. McMillan. Boulder, Col.: Lynne Rienner Publishers.

Sinclair, A., and J. Fryxell. 1985. The Sahel of Africa: Ecology of a Disaster. *Canadian Journal of Zoology* 63:987–94.

Smith, M., S. Paulsen, W. Fougere, and S. Ritchey. 1983. Socioeconomic, Educational and Health Factors Influencing Growth of Rural Haitian Children. *Ecology of Food and Nutrition* 13:99–108.

Spencer, P. 1965. *The Samburu: A Study of Gerontocracy in a Nomadic Tribe.* Berkeley and Los Angeles: University of California Press.

———. 1973. *Nomads in Alliance: Symbiosis and Growth Among the Rendille and Samburu of Kenya.* London: Oxford University Press.

Spring, A., C. Smith, and F. Kayuni. 1983. Women Farmers in Malawi: Their Contributions to Agriculture and Participation in Development Projects. Chitedze, Malawi: Women in Development Project.

Staatz, J. 1979. *The Economics of Cattle and Meat Marketing in the Ivory Coast.* Livestock Production and Marketing in the Entente States of West Africa, Monograph No. 2. Ann Arbor: University of Michigan, Center for Research on Economic Development.

Stanford, M. 1989. *Export Agriculture and the Mexican Farmer: The Case of Melon Production in Apatzingan, Michoacan.* Ann Arbor, Mich.: University Microfilms.

Stremplat, A. 1981. The Impact of Food Aid and Food Security Programmes on Development in Recipient Countries. Schriften des Zentrums fur Regionale Entwicklungsforshung der Justus Leibig Universitat Gieben. Vol. 19. Saarbrucken-Fort Lauderdale: Verlag Breitenbach Publishers.

Swaminathan, M. 1984. Nutrition and Agricultural Development: New Frontiers. *Food and Nutrition* 10:33–41.

Timmer, C., W. Falcon, and S. Pearson. 1983. *Food Policy Analysis*. Baltimore: Johns Hopkins University Press for the World Bank.

Torry, W. 1973. *Subsistence Ecology Among the Gabra: Nomads of the Kenya/ Ethiopia Frontier*. Ph.D. diss., Columbia University.

Trapnell, C. G., and J. N. Clothier. 1936. *The Soils, Vegetation and Agricultural Systems of North-Western Rhodesia*. Lusaka: Government Printers.

Tripp, R. 1982. Farmers and Traders: Some Economic Determinants of Nutritional Status in Northern Ghana. *Food and Nutrition Bulletin* 8:3–11.

———. 1984. On Farm Research and Applied Nutrition: Some Suggestions for Collaboration Between National Institutes of Nutrition and Agricultural Research. *Food and Nutrition Bulletin* 6:49–57.

United Nations. 1989. *World Economic Survey 1989: Current Trends and Policies in the World Economy*. New York: Department of International and Social Affairs.

United States Agency for International Development (USAID). 1984a. Congressional Presentation Fiscal Year 1984. Washington, D.C.: USAID.

———. 1984b. *Africa Bureau: Nutrition Guidelines for Agriculture and Rural Development*. Washington, D.C.: USAID.

———. 1986. Annual Report of the Chairman of the Development Coordination Committee, Annex 2. Washington, D.C. USAID.

United States Department of Agriculture (USDA). 1981. Food for Peace: 1979 Annual Report on Public Law 480. Washington, D.C.: U.S. Government Printing Office.

———. 1981. U.S. Trade in Livestock and Products Declined in 1980. *Foreign Agriculture Circular—Livestock and Meat*. FLM-MT-4-81 (February). Washington, D.C.: U.S. Government Printing Office.

United States Department of Justice, Immigration and Naturalization Service. 1987. Statistical Yearbook of Immigration and Naturalization. Washington, D.C.: U.S. Government Printing Office.

United States 83rd Congress. 1954. Public Law 480, July 10, 1954. Statutes at Large: 83d Congress, 2d Session. Washington, D.C.: U.S. Government Printing Office.

United States 87th Congress, Joint Economic Committee. 1962. Economic Policies and Programs in South America. Subcommittee on InterAmerican Economic Relationships. Washington, D.C.: U.S. Government Printing Office.

United States House of Representatives. 1989. Subcommittee on Appropriations, Foreign Operations, Export Financing and Related Programs. Appropriations for 1989. Washington, D.C.: U.S. Government Printing Office.

United States House of Representatives, Foreign Affairs Committee. 1970, 1973, 1976, 1979, 1981. U.S. Overseas Loans and Grants and Assistance from International Organizations. Washington, D.C.: U.S. Government Printing Office.

United States International Trade Commission. 1986. Certain Fresh Cut Flowers from Canada, Chile, Colombia, Costa Rica, Ecuador, Israel, Kenya, Mexico and Peru. Investigation Nos. 303 TA-17, July 18, 1986. (Microfiche #9886-19.49 &.50).

United States Presidential Commission on World Hunger. 1980. Overcoming World Hunger: The Challenge Ahead. Washington, D.C.: U.S. Government Printing Office.

Uquillas, J., C. Crissman, W. Peterson, and K. DeWalt. 1988. *Potatoes in Farming Systems of Highland Ecuador.* Fundacion para Desarrollo Agropecuario (FUNDAGRO) Working Paper Series. Quito, Ecuador: FUNDAGRO.

Valdes. 1983. Integrating Nutrition into Agricultural Policy. In *Nutrition Intervention Strategies in National Development,* ed. B. A. Underwood. New York: Academic Press.

Wade, N. 1974. Green Revolution (II): Problems of Adapting a Western Technology. *Science* 186:1186–92.

Wallerstein, M. 1980. *Food for War—Food for Peace: United States Food Aid in a Global Context.* Cambridge: M.I.T. Press.

Wellhausen, E. 1976. The Agriculture of Mexico. *Scientific American* 235: 128–50.

Whitehead, A. 1981. "I'm Hungry, Mum": The Politics of Domestic Budgeting. In *Of Marriage and the Market,* ed. K. Young, C. Wolkowitz, and R. McCullagh. London: CSE Books.

World Bank. 1981. *Accelerated Development in Sub-Saharan Africa: An Agenda for Action.* Washington, D.C.: World Bank.

———. 1983. World Development Report 1983. New York: Oxford University Press.

———. 1987. World Development Report 1987. New York: Oxford University Press.

———. 1988. Social Indicators of Development 1988. Baltimore and London: Johns Hopkins University Press.

————. 1989. World Development Report 1989. New York: Oxford University Press.

Worsley, P. 1962. *The Third World*. London: Weidenfeld and Nicolson.

Yates, P. 1981. *Mexico's Agricultural Dilemma*. Tucson: University of Arizona Press.

Contributors

ROBERTA D. BAER is an assistant professor of anthropology at the University of South Florida. Her research interests include food policy and nutritional anthropology, cross-cultural health care systems and use of folk remedies. She has conducted field research in Mexico, western South America, India, and the United States.

DAVID BARKIN is a professor of economics at the Universidad Autónoma Metropolitana—Xochimilco and an investigator in the Centro de Ecodesarrollo (Ecodevelopment Center) in Mexico City. His publications include *Regional Economic Development in Mexico* (with Timothy King) and *Food Crops Versus Feed Crops: The Substitution of Grains in World Production* (with Rosemary Batt and Billie DeWalt).

BILLIE R. DEWALT is chair of the Department of Anthropology at the University of Kentucky and holds appointments as a professor of anthropology and sociology and in the Patterson School of Diplomacy. His research interests include agricultural anthropology, food policy, and political economy. He is a coeditor of the series *Food Systems and Agrarian Change* for Cornell University Press.

KATHLEEN M. DEWALT is an associate professor of behavioral science and anthropology at the University of Kentucky. Her research interests have focused on the nutritional impact of agricultural change in several Latin American countries and on the social factors that affect dietary behavior. She is currently involved in a project designed to assist agricultural projects in including food consumption and nutrition goals in their work and in two research projects examining dietary behavior in rural communities in Kentucky. She is the author of *Nutritional Strategies and Agricultural Change*.

PAUL L. DOUGHTY is a professor of anthropology and Latin American studies at the University of Florida. He has worked in development and applied anthropology projects in Mexico, Central America, and Peru, and has provided development evaluation and consultant work for USAID, the

Peace Corps, and other international agencies. Currently he serves as co-chair of the Society for Latin American Anthropology and executive secretary for the Commission on the Study of Peace of the International Union of Anthropological and Ethnological Sciences and as editor of its quarterly publication, *Human Peace*.

ART HANSEN is an associate professor of anthropology at the University of Florida. His research and development experience has focused on Latin America and Africa. He has consulted for USAID, the United Nations Development Fund, and the World Bank in farming systems research. He is a coeditor of *Food in Sub-Saharan Africa* and *Involuntary Migration and Settlement*.

JEANNE HARLOW is a project coordinator for Tropical Research and Development, a private consulting firm in Gainesville, Florida. She has worked extensively in technical writing and multimedia presentations, with an emphasis on agriculture and a concentration on Africa.

J. TERRANCE MCCABE holds a joint appointment in the Department of Anthropology and the Institute of Behavioral Science at the University of Colorado. He has served in the Peace Corps in Sierra Leone working in agricultural extension and has conducted various field projects among the Turkana in Kenya and the Masai in Tanzania in cooperation with various international development and conservation agencies. He is a coeditor of *South Turkana Nomadism: Coping with an Unpredictably Varying Environment*.

DELLA E. MCMILLAN is the deputy director of a joint World Bank–United Nations Development Program project to review settlement-related development in the eleven-country area in West Africa covered by the Onchocerciasis Control Program. She is an assistant professor of anthropology at the University of Kentucky and the former director of the Food in Africa Program at the University of Florida, where she was also the assistant director of the Center for African Studies. She is also a coeditor of *Food in Sub-Saharan Africa*.

EDWARD B. REEVES is an associate professor of sociology and anthropology at Morehead State University. He has served as field director of the INTSORMIL/University of Kentucky Farming Systems Research Project in North Kordofan, Sudan, and as a consultant on additional projects in the Sudan. His current research interests are divided between political rituals and power structure and agricultural and rural development. He is a coeditor (with Sheldon Smith) of *Human Systems Ecology* and the author of *The Hidden Government: Ritual, Clientelism, and Legitimation in Northern Egypt.*

SOUTHERN ANTHROPOLOGICAL SOCIETY PROCEEDINGS

Nos. 1–4, 6–7, 10–11 are out of print.

No. 5, *Red, White, and Black: Symposium on Indians in the Old South,* edited by Charles M. Hudson.

No. 8, *Social and Cultural Identity: Problems of Persistence and Change,* edited by Thomas K. Fitzgerald.

No. 9, *Symbols and Society: Essays on Belief Systems in Action,* edited by Carole E. Hill.

No. 12, *Interethnic Communication,* edited by E. Lamar Ross.

No. 13, *Predicting Sociocultural Change,* edited by Susan Abbott and John van Willigen.

No. 14, *Cities in a Larger Context,* edited by Thomas W. Collins.

No. 15, *Holding on to the Land and the Lord: Kinship, Ritual, Land Tenure, and Social Policy in the Rural South,* edited by Robert L. Hall and Carol B. Stack.

No. 16, *Bilingualism: Social Issues and Policy Implications,* edited by Andrew W. Miracle.

No. 17, *Cultural Adaptation to Mountain Environments,* edited by Patricia D. Beaver and Burton L. Purrington.

No. 18, *The Burden of Being Civilized: An Anthropological Perspective on the Discontents of Civilization,* edited by Miles Richardson and Malcolm C. Webb.

No. 19, *Current Health Policy Issues and Alternatives: An Applied Social Science Perspective,* edited by Carole E. Hill.

No. 20, *Visions and Revisions: Ethnohistoric Perspectives on Southern Cultures,* edited by George Sabo III and William M. Schneider.

No. 21, *Sea and Land: Cultural and Biological Adaptations in the Southern Coastal Plain,* edited by James L. Peacock and James C. Sabella.

No. 22, *Women in the South: An Anthropological Perspective,* edited by Holly F. Mathews.

No. 23, *Cultural Heritage Conservation in the American South,* edited by Benita J. Howell.

No. 24, *Anthropology and Food Policy: Human Dimensions of Food Policy in Africa and Latin America,* edited by Della E. McMillan. With the assistance of Jeanne Harlow.

Index to Southern Anthropological Society Proceedings, Volumes 1–10, prepared by John J. Honigmann and Irma Honigmann.